Do you ever feel "less-than" i[n] of your life that you keep hi[dden] happen if they really knew yo[u] performance, trying to compensate for your weaknesses? If so, you've come to the right place! In this honest and beautifully written book, Esther Liu serves as a trustworthy and humble guide for fellow strugglers who yearn for freedom from the shackles of shame. With care and compassion, she walks the reader through a deeper understanding of the multifaceted experience of shame and points repeatedly to its glorious reversal in our lives through our shame-bearing Savior, Jesus Christ.

—**Michael R. Emlet**, Dean of Faculty and Counselor, Christian Counseling & Educational Foundation (CCEF); Author, *Saints, Sufferers, and Sinners*

Esther Liu gently helps us to push into the dark and hard spaces of our lives in order to bring us closer to our Savior. If you or someone you love struggles with shame, you will be helped and equipped by the tender truths of Scripture that Esther has compiled. This book has already ministered to my soul, and I'm eager to see how her work will be used to help others to know the love and nearness of Christ.

—**Jonathan D. Holmes**, Executive Director, Fieldstone Counseling

Esther Liu captures with pinpoint precision the pervasive voice of shame and the perfect Christ who absolves and restores us from the verdicts we often place on ourselves and have placed on us by others. Esther declares with empathy and authority that the voice of shame is overcome by the grace and love of Christ. The daily readings articulate perfectly what many pilgrims have been thinking but have been afraid to say aloud. This beautiful, unveiling devotional vividly shows the power of confronting wounds as it exhorts us toward the healing that awaits us in Christ.

—**Peter Ong**, Program Manager for Community Engagement, Redeemer City to City; Ministry Director, Living Faith Community Church (PCA)

Esther Liu tenderly holds out God's heart for shame-filled people who are unsure if his love extends to them. *Shame* is filled with inviting passages, practical reflections, and precious stories of Esther's struggle with shame. If you wrestle with shame, you will feel known and cared for by Esther as she invites you into the hope that Jesus will meet and help you amid your struggle.

—**Darby A. Strickland**, Counselor, Christian Counseling & Educational Foundation (CCEF); Author, *Is It Abuse?*

You may enter this devotional with a sense that you are worthless—and who doesn't feel that way?—or it may be more pointed: "You are disgusting." Either way, open this book and read the first two days. You will, like me, keep reading.

—**Edward T. Welch**, Faculty and Counselor, Christian Counseling & Educational Foundation (CCEF); Author, *Shame Interrupted*

S H A M E

31-Day Devotionals for Life

A Series

Deepak Reju
Series Editor

SHAME

BEING
KNOWN AND
LOVED

ESTHER LIU

P U B L I S H I N G

P.O. BOX 817 • PHILLIPSBURG • NEW JERSEY 08865-0817

To David Powlison:

The legacy of your ministry and love
is found on every page of this book,
and I would have it no other way.
Thank you for everything.

© 2022 by Esther Liu

All rights reserved. No part of this book may be reproduced, stored in a retrieval system, or transmitted in any form or by any means—electronic, mechanical, photocopy, recording, or otherwise—except for brief quotations for the purpose of review or comment, without the prior permission of the publisher, P&R Publishing Company, P.O. Box 817, Phillipsburg, New Jersey 08865-0817.

Scripture quotations are from the ESV® Bible (The Holy Bible, English Standard Version®), copyright © 2001 by Crossway, a publishing ministry of Good News Publishers. Used by permission. All rights reserved.

A Scripture quotation from the New Testament uses the ESV's alternate, footnoted translation of *adelphoi* ("brothers and sisters").

Italics within Scripture quotations indicate emphasis added.

Printed in the United States of America

Library of Congress Cataloging-in-Publication Data

Names: Liu, Esther, author.
Title: Shame : being known and loved / Esther Liu.
Description: Phillipsburg, New Jersey : P&R Publishing, [2022] | Series: 31-day devotionals for life | Summary: "Do you feel weighed down by shame-a painful sense of deficiency and failure? In thirty-one devotional readings, biblical counselor Esther Liu leads you to discover lasting hope and comfort"-- Provided by publisher.
Identifiers: LCCN 2022018995 | ISBN 9781629950020 (paperback) | ISBN 9781629950082 (epub)
Subjects: LCSH: Shame--Religious aspects--Christianity. | Shame--Biblical teaching. | Devotional literature.
Classification: LCC BT714 .L58 2022 | DDC 296.7/2--dc23/eng/20220512
LC record available at https://lccn.loc.gov/2022018995

Contents

What Now?

How to Nourish Your Soul

A LITTLE BIT every day can do great good for your soul.

I read the Bible to my kids during breakfast. I don't read a lot. Maybe just a few verses. But I work hard to do it every weekday.

My wife and I pray for one of our children, a different child each night, before we go to bed. We usually take just a few minutes. We don't pray lengthy, expansive prayers. But we try to do this most every night.

Although they don't take long, these practices are edifying, hopeful, and effective.

This devotional is just the same. Each entry is short. Just a few tasty morsels of Scripture to nourish your hungry soul. Read it on the subway or the bus on the way to work. Read it with a friend or a spouse every night at dinner. Make it a part of each day for thirty-one days, and it will do you great good.

Why is that?

We start with Scripture. God's Word is powerful. Used by the Holy Spirit, it turns the hearts of kings, brings comfort to the lowly, and gives spiritual sight to the blind. It transforms lives and turns them upside down. We know that the Bible is God's very own words, so we read and study it to know God himself.

Our study of Scripture is practical. Theology should change how we live. It's crucial to connect the Word with your struggles. Often, as you read this devotional, you'll see the word *you* because Esther speaks directly to you, the reader. Each reading contains a reflection question and practical suggestion. You'll get much more from this experience if you answer the questions and do the practical exercises. Don't skip them. Do them for the sake of your own soul.

Our study of Scripture is worshipful. Shame plagues us like a sickness that can't be shaken or like a dark, stormy cloud that follows us around. It's a painful experience. We can feel exposed, rejected, and dirty. We can feel like failures. Shame keeps us distant from others, especially those whose help we desperately need. Yet, for the believer, there is hope. Christ came for those who are filled with shame. The Holy One covers the naked, accepts the outcast, cleanses the unclean, and comforts those who have failed. We see the great Rescuer of our souls in God's Word, and he reorients our worship. Shame no longer takes center stage in our hearts. Christ does. We embrace God's Word because it points the ashamed to Christ as our one true sufficient foundation.

If you find this devotional helpful (and I trust that you will!), reread it in different seasons of your life. Work through it this coming month, then come back to it a year from now to remind yourself that ultimately you are known and loved by God in Christ.

If, after reading and rereading Esther's devotional, you want more gospel-rich resources to help you with your shame, she has listed several at the end of the book. Buy them and make good use of them.

Are you ready? Let's begin.

Deepak Reju

Introduction

THIS BOOK WAS almost not written.

That's probably a strange way to start a book, but it is true. And I make this confession because it is relevant here. This book was almost not written because of shame. It was almost not written because I, the author, felt disqualified to write it. I didn't feel gifted enough, wise enough, insightful enough, disciplined enough, skilled enough, spiritual enough. *Who do I think I am? I am a nobody. Why would anyone want to read what I write? I have nothing worthwhile to offer. Why waste everyone's time? Why even try?* On and on it went in my mind—the self-doubt, the self-condemnation, the persistent nagging voice that whispered in my ear and breathed down my neck, leaving me paralyzed and defeated.

This is a snapshot of shame. This is a snapshot of what many of us experience on a regular basis to varying degrees, even if we're not trying to write a book. We hear the self-doubting, self-loathing voice at work, in school, or at church. It emerges in social situations, in romantic relationships, and in our homes. It creeps into our consciousness when the busyness of our day slows down enough to leave us with our own thoughts.

It is the voice that says you're not enough because of the way you look—because of your weight, your build, or the color of your skin. It is the voice that says you're not enough because you are still single instead of married with kids. Because you've always been different from others, never fitting in.

It is the voice that says you're not enough because of the things you've done in your past. Because of the things you did and struggled with *today*. Because of the things other people have done *to* you—things that left you feeling dirty and worthless.

It is the voice that says you're not enough because rejection or failure is all you've known in life. Because you didn't come from the right kind of family. Because you failed to meet the expectations that others, including God, have placed on you—or the expectations that you placed on yourself. Because somewhere along the line you began to internalize the damaging words your parent spoke about you when you were a child. Or perhaps it was the *nothingness* you internalized: the experience of being invisible, unheard, neglected, treated with apathy, and overlooked— accumulated evidence that you don't matter.

It is the voice that says you're not enough because when you look at other people, they don't seem to struggle the way you do. Other people are put-together, happy, productive, successful, competent, sociable, popular, loved, sanctified, fruitful—and you are simply . . . not. So not only do you not feel good enough, but you feel *alone* in not being good enough. You have a sense of deficiency—a feeling that something is wrong with you, that you're the problem—and a sense of isolation.

Shame can be painful. It can be crippling. For some of us, it is life-consuming.

What are we to do with our shame? This devotional seeks to begin to answer this question. The operative word here is *begin*. We will not be completely free from the shackles of shame by the end of our thirty-one days together. We will not have it all figured out. Shame is complex and multifaceted. There are no simplistic or trite solutions and no quick fixes. Yet, as we dig into Scripture together, I hope you will see that there *are* answers, answers that matter, answers that I pray will make a meaningful difference in your life and set you on a different trajectory.

I write this devotional as a counselor at the Christian Counseling & Educational Foundation (CCEF) in Pennsylvania. I have been privileged to walk alongside many people who have entrusted their lives and burdens to me. Shame comes up often. Whether the presenting problem is depression, anxiety, addiction, anger, relational challenges, singleness, OCD . . . shame is often close by. The reflections in this book are the fruit of those precious conversations over the years, the fruit of considering together what God has to say to shame-filled souls.

I also write this devotional as a fellow struggler. Shame has been one of the most stubborn struggles of my life. I am well acquainted with the voice of self-condemnation and the sting of rejection. I am acquainted with the anxious, desperate resolve to do better, to *be* better—and with what it feels like for my best to ultimately not be enough. I am acquainted with self-protection, hiding, and image management.

All this to say, I do not speak merely as one who has professionally helped others through shame. I also speak as someone who has been profoundly *helped* in my own struggle with shame—by a merciful and kind God and by loved ones who have reflected that mercy and kindness to me.

Before we begin, here are some orienting thoughts and suggestions for how you can use this devotional:

- *Please pace yourself.* The reflections may surface painful emotions and memories. Give yourself permission to take breaks, to go through a reflection every other day, once a week—whatever feels wisest and most manageable for you.
- *Consider inviting someone to pray for you*—or even to read the book with you. Shame is inherently isolating. It is no surprise that we often find grace and mercy in the context of safe and wise relationships.
- *Take opportunities to apply what you read*—to allow the material to soak into your heart and meaningfully (and slowly) rearrange your life. You may find it helpful to use a journal or start a computer document to jot down your thoughts.

When all is said and done, there is hope for our shame-filled souls. We are about to embark on a journey to discover that hope.

We will discover that it's not found in a set of principles or strategies, nor is it found in ourselves. We will find that our ultimate and lasting hope is in a Person. A Person who has determined that shame, unworthiness, and rejection will not have final say in our lives. A Person who was willing to do everything and sacrifice everything, even his very life, to make it so. Lord and Savior, please make it so.

OUR SHAME

Shame often lurks in the shadows. It can be easier to identify anxiety, depression, workaholism, anger, or addiction in our lives than to see the shame that often accompanies these experiences. We may struggle with perfectionism, burnout, hopelessness, escapism, self-harm...the list goes on—and overlook the underlying sense of unworthiness.

Shame thrives in darkness, so our first step in the journey toward hope is to identify and put words to it. When we better understand our shame, and grow in speaking about it to God and others, we begin to discover the light of life.

DAY 1

Beginning with the End

"Behold, the dwelling place of God is with man. . . . He will wipe away every tear from their eyes, and death shall be no more, neither shall there be mourning, nor crying, nor pain anymore, for the former things have passed away." (Rev. 21:3–4)

DEAR BELIEVER, as we begin, please know this journey may be hard. I'll be inviting you to think about things you would probably prefer not to think about. So I begin with the end to give you a glimpse of where we're heading—so you know we won't do this hard, messy work in vain.

Today's passage describes a day when God will dwell with you. He will come near to tenderly wipe away every tear from your eyes. Mourning, crying, and pain will be no more. Shame will not have the final say in your life.

Imagine a day when there will be no more painful self-consciousness or envious comparing of yourself to others—you will be free to love and serve courageously. No more hamster wheel of trying to prove yourself—you will be wholly able to enjoy the Lord and experience his enjoyment of you. No more exclusion, isolation, and rejection—he will be with you forevermore. No more sins, failures, or regrets—the former things will pass away. No more self-loathing, dark secrets, or anxious striving. All that will remain will be joy, belonging, intimacy, light, goodness, radiance, beauty, rest, life.

This may sound too good to be true, and that's okay. For now, even a glimmer of possibility is enough.

Have you ever watched an action movie where the tension ramps up so high that it feels hopeless? The enemy has the upper hand; the situation is bleak. Yet what happens if you watch the movie having read the spoilers beforehand? You experience it differently. No matter what happens, no matter how many good people are killed, no matter how hopeless it seems, you know that good will prevail.

Today's passage is the spoiler for our lives. How our journey with shame ends isn't something that could go either way. God wins. Through Christ's death and resurrection, we win. Closeness, intimacy, light, and radiance win. We need that assurance. We need hope that despite the tangled knots of shame—despite what feels dark, irredeemable, and insoluble—good will prevail for us too. Even if we can't see it now. Even if we can't imagine how. Even if today it feels like the opposite is true. That is what today's passage holds out for us.

In counseling, the first session can be the hardest. Counselees come in and explain what led them to seek help. As they hear themselves speak, despair sinks in. "This is a lot. This is too much . . ."

"But you're here," I often say. "God led you to get help. He led you to this counseling room. Perhaps this is his way of letting you know he is pursuing you and already at work."

I wonder if the same is true here. You could be doing a million other things. But you're reading this devotional. Perhaps God is letting you know that he intends to bring about redemption in the broken, shameful pieces of your life.

There is hard work ahead. But knowing God is already at work, knowing what he is ultimately working toward, may we find an ounce of courage to enter in.

Reflect: Do you feel defeated or skeptical as you start this devotional? Hopeful? Scared to hope? How does today's reading affect you?

Act: Express how you are feeling to God. Ask him to meet you where you are. Write out a prayer if you'd like.

DAY 2

What Is Your Story?

So when the woman saw that the tree was good for food . . . she
took of its fruit and ate, and she also gave some to her husband
who was with her, and he ate. Then the eyes of both were opened,
and they knew that they were naked. And they sewed fig leaves
together and made themselves loincloths. (Gen. 3:6–7)

"I'm proud of you." Andrew had longed to hear these words
from his father growing up, but nothing he did had ever seemed
like enough. Though he was now a successful, well-respected
businessman, no amount of achievement, affirmation, wealth, or
status could erase his lingering sense of unworthiness.

"No godly man will ever want to marry me." Hannah lost her
virginity to a man she thought would be her future husband, but
he betrayed and left her. Her self-loathing was all that remained.

Two stories of shame.

Here is another. A man and a woman were in a garden. All was
well. Genesis 2:25 makes a point of saying they "were both naked
and were not ashamed." Yet we're familiar with the story: a forbidden tree, a serpent's deception. The fruit looked good; the woman
ate it. The man ate it too. Suddenly they went from "naked and not
ashamed" to covering themselves with fig leaves because they were
very ashamed. The human tendency to cover ourselves up before
others has been passed down for generations, all the way to us.

What can we learn about shame from these stories?

First, shame involves other people. Andrew longed for
approval from his father. Hannah despaired that no godly man
would ever want her. Shame led Adam and Eve to hide their bod-
ies from each other and from God. Each of us have characters in
our stories of shame.

Second, shame involves standards. Adam and Eve felt shame after they violated God's command not to eat from the forbidden tree. They had fallen short of his standards. Like Adam and Eve, Andrew, and Hannah, we too feel shame when we fail to meet certain standards—whether they be God's commands, the expectations of our parents or friends, or cultural norms. We use all kinds of standards as criteria to evaluate ourselves and our worth, and we experience shame when we fall short.

Here are some questions to consider:

- What is *your* story of shame?
- What particular life experiences brought you to this devotional?
- Whose opinions have really mattered to you in the past?
- Whose approval do you seek today, or whose disapproval do you fear?
- In what areas are you tempted to strive to prove yourself?
- What standards do you fail to meet?

I invite you to name specifics, because God intends for this journey to be personal. He speaks to *you*—to *your* story. He knows the particular people and standards that have made your shame so sticky. His mercies meet you in your specific insecurities and heartaches. He promises to help. As you begin to identify the particulars of your shame story, would you speak to him and invite his help?

Reflect: Choose one question to answer from the bulleted list above. Refrain from making moral evaluations of right or wrong—your only goal for now is to identify more particulars.

Act: Write down two to three standards to which you often hold yourself but that you fail to meet. As you think of additional ones in the coming days, you can add to your list.

DAY 3

"I Must Hide"

*The man and his wife hid themselves from the presence of the
Lord God among the trees of the garden. But the Lord God
called to the man and said to him, "Where are you?" And he
said, "I heard the sound of you in the garden, and I was afraid,
because I was naked, and I hid myself." (Gen. 3:8–10)*

When we look for shame, we look for areas in our lives
where we are tempted to conceal, to cover up, to pretend:

- An eleven-year-old boy schemes of ways to hide his school
  grades from his parents, dreading their disappointment.
- A victim of childhood sexual abuse avoids disclosing her
  past to her friends, afraid they will be disgusted by her
  "baggage."
- A man learns to bottle up his emotions, having been taught
  from a young age that boys don't cry and emotions are a
  sign of weakness.
- A woman chooses clothes that will conceal the extra
  pounds she has gained.
- A married couple smiles brightly at church on Sundays
  and on social media, pretending everything is okay when
  their lives are falling apart behind closed doors.

Many of us pretend we are more okay than we are. We present to others only what we want them to see. Why? Because we
fear that people will discover the ugly and unlovable parts of us
and then reject us. We struggle alone because we are not ready to
bear the risks of confession, disclosure, and honesty. Shame com-
plicates and erodes our relationships—including our relationship

with God. Hence Adam's words: "I heard the sound of you in the garden, and I was afraid."

Tim Keller wrote, "To be loved but not known is comforting but superficial. To be known and not loved is our greatest fear. But to be fully known and truly loved . . . is what we need more than anything."[1]

The reality is that relationships are hard and messy. They can be marked by anxiety. Many of us have settled for "comforting but superficial" in our relationships. Yet Keller's quote points us to a richer possibility: maybe vulnerability and intimacy can feel safe and life-giving again, as they did for Adam and Eve before they sinned. Maybe we can find a way out of all the hiding—a way we can taste the joy of being fully known and truly loved.

"You're the first person I've ever told . . ." When a counselee says this to me, it doesn't matter what confession follows. I know that moment is Spirit-wrought victory: a glorious movement from darkness to light, from isolation to community, from secrecy and hiding to freedom and new life. It is heroic and admirable—a glimpse of what God intends our lives and relationships to be. We will see later in the devotional how God brings this intention to fruition in Jesus Christ.

Reflect: What do you tend to hide from others? What parts of your story or facets of your personality do you wish to remain unknown? What are some present-day struggles you have a hard time sharing with others?

Act: Consider what hiding strategies you use in your relationships. Do you lie or exaggerate? Avoid disclosing emotions and struggles? Write down one or two ways you tend to hide, cover up, or pretend.

DAY 4

"There's Something Wrong with Me"

Now Laban had two daughters. The name of the older was Leah, and the name of the younger was Rachel. Leah's eyes were weak, but Rachel was beautiful in form and appearance. Jacob loved Rachel. (Gen. 29:16–18)

TODAY'S PASSAGE SETS up a contrast that shame strugglers can likely resonate with. "Leah's eyes were weak, but Rachel was beautiful in form and appearance. Jacob loved Rachel."

Here with Leah we can begin to differentiate between guilt and shame. Guilt says, "I *did* something wrong," whereas shame says, "*I* am wrong; there's something wrong with me." "Weak eyes" doesn't convey a sense that Leah was *doing* anything wrong. Yet something was wrong with her. She failed to measure up to a certain standard, and Jacob's love went to Rachel instead. This is not a matter of guilt . . . but it is very much a matter of shame.

If you struggle with shame, you're likely wrestling with your own version of "weak eyes." It could be related to your physical appearance, social skills, or résumé. It could be tied to past mistakes or the messiness of your life today. Whatever standard you hold yourself to—if you have compared yourself to others and come up short, been overlooked, or been left behind—this story is for you. If you've ever felt unvalued and unlovable, this story is for you.

We are still in Genesis, but already shame is everywhere. Even if the word is not explicitly mentioned, the Bible is about shame. It is about the experience of unworthiness, the pain of rejection, the isolating sense of not being good enough. It is about people (in this case, Jacob) who evaluate and assess lovability. It is about standards that determine worth or lack of worth (in this case, Rachel's physical beauty and Leah's weak eyes).

Sometimes we're not even sure what our "weak eyes" are. Our shame may emerge from some mental reverse engineering. When we are repeatedly overlooked and rejected, we are tempted to conclude there must be something wrong with us, even if we're not sure what it is. When we are overwhelmed by hardship and suffering, we can begin to wonder if God is displeased with us, if we are second-class Christians in his eyes. "There must be something wrong with me—or else my life wouldn't look like this."

What are we doing today? We are continuing to locate stories of shame in the Bible. We are allowing Scripture to expand our vocabulary for shame, to help us articulate our own shame experiences. Do you resonate with Leah and her "weak eyes"? Do you wish you could be more like Rachel instead? God's Word does not fly high above these experiences but is utterly realistic in depicting what life on this side of heaven can look and feel like— what shame can look and feel like. God gets it. And as we progress through Scripture, we'll see he has every intention to do something about it too.

Reflect: What is one thing you often feel insecure about? What is one way you often compare yourself to others?

Act: Write down a one-sentence prayer expressing your insecurity. "God, I struggle with _____." If you have a trusted companion, consider sharing with them.

DAY 5

"I'll Try Harder"

And Leah conceived and bore a son, and she called his name Reuben,
*for she said, "Because the L*ORD *has looked upon my affliction;*
for now my husband will love me." She conceived again and bore
*a son, and said, "Because the L*ORD *has heard that I am hated,*
he has given me this son also." . . . Again she conceived and bore
a son, and said, "Now this time my husband will be attached to
me, because I have borne him three sons." (Gen. 29:32–34)

MY COUNSELEE STRUGGLED with an eating disorder. Sophia would binge, then purge. When she gained weight, she punished herself by skipping meals and slavishly exercising. She wanted to be loved. She wanted to be beautiful—but she never quite lived up to her standards.

Can you relate to Sophia? "If only I could be more this, or that, I could become worthy." More physically attractive. More self-disciplined. More intelligent. Or less emotional. Less awkward. Less needy.

The logic makes sense initially. If you struggle with shame because of X, Y, Z, then the solution to get rid of shame is to fix X, Y, Z.

Counselor and teacher David Powlison likened this to climbing ladders. Each ladder represents a standard we live by, whether it be physical beauty, intelligence, ministry success, or something else.[1] The higher you are on the ladder, the better you feel about yourself. The lower you are, the more you feel resigned to a lesser, shame-filled life. We tend to look at the people above us on our ladders and feel self-condemnation or envy. We look at the people far below us and feel superior, even judgmental. We look at the people right under us and worry that they might surpass us.

23

In today's passage, we see that Leah was also climbing a ladder. Back then, a woman's worth was found in childbearing. Leah was convinced that the more children she bore, the more likely her husband would be to love her. "Now my husband will love me . . . now this time my husband will love me . . ." and on and on it went.

We can be convinced that reaching the top of a particular ladder is the solution to our shame and will earn us the gains we desperately long for: love, acceptance, self-worth, significance. So we push ourselves; we try harder. We feel the pressure to do better and be better—to keep climbing. All the while, we are anxious and insecure. We are threatened by others' successes. We are arrogant and self-righteous or envious and discouraged. We are weighed down and weary.

We will see tomorrow that ladder-climbing doesn't ultimately deliver on its promises. It doesn't provide true and abiding freedom, peace, and contentment—even if you reach the top. That's why Powlison calls these "the ladders to nowhere."[2] That's why I often call ladder-climbing "the ladder game of hell"—because there is something hellish about this self-reliant, anxious striving that does not ultimately rescue you from shame.

But for today, our goal is to identify where we may be trying to prove and improve ourselves to escape shame. We want to consider the ways ladder-climbing has left us weary and anxious. We begin to pray for another way.

Reflect: Consider what ladders you are tempted to climb. The ladders of academic, career, or family success? The ladders of personality, giftedness, status? If you're unsure, consider the areas in which you struggle with envy, comparison, or self-righteousness in your life.

Act: As you go through your day, see if you can identify any moments of ladder-climbing. Write down your observations.

DAY 6

A Glimpse of a Better Way

[Leah] conceived again and bore a son, and said, "This time I will praise the LORD." Therefore she called his name Judah. Then she ceased bearing. (Gen. 29:35)

SOME OF US are working hard to climb ladders but are losing hope. Some of us have given up, resigned to our shame. Others of us may have made it relatively high on our ladders, only to find our sense of insecurity isn't cured up there. When Sophia (see day 5) reached her ideal weight last summer, she was exhilarated at first. But her anxiety quickly returned. She now felt overwhelming pressure to *maintain* her weight loss. She started to wonder if she would be prettier if she lost another five pounds. After trying so hard to reach the top, she realized there were more ladder rungs to climb.

As we saw in yesterday's passage, Leah tried to climb a ladder too. Three sons for Jacob—a respectable number in ancient Near Eastern society. But the first son didn't give her what she sought, because she was still looking for Jacob's love with the second son . . . and the third. The lack of love she received was not for lack of effort.

What do you do when climbing ladders doesn't work? What hope is left for you when your best efforts are not enough?

In today's passage, we witness a transformation in Leah. Something happens between verse 34 and verse 35. When she gives birth to her fourth son, she no longer fixates on Jacob's love. Jacob is noticeably absent from her post-birth speech. What used to be "Now my husband will love me" turns into "This time I will praise the LORD."

Do you want to know the source of hope for your shame-filled soul? Do you want to find a way that is better than your ladder games? From Leah's transformation, we begin to see that knowing God, being in relationship with him, and praising him help us to step off our ladders to nowhere.

Some of you have tried really hard with these ladders. Perhaps you will resonate with these words I wrote years ago and called "An Ode to the Nobodies":

> when you feel overlooked & unimportant
> when hopes for success are met with strings of failure
> when you're lost in the sea of dull mediocrity while others sparkle
> when earnest efforts amount to nothingness and futility
> useless, ugly, not enough
> when all of it tempts you to give up . . .
> I pray you would know
> it is a mercy to not thrive in a game you can't win.

This was my feeble prayer for myself in a dark season of shame—that I would see I was playing a futile game I could never win. Maybe I would finally have the sanity to step off the ladder. I prayed to see the goodness of God in my thwarted ambitions so that I could find a better way to live. So that I could find *him*. And as I continue praying these things for myself, I pray these same things for you. May he redirect the eyes of our hearts to him. That is where we will look in the next section.

Reflect: Have you ever experienced the futility of playing the ladder game? Describe what ladder you were climbing and why it didn't work for you.

Act: Write a prayer that asks God to help you to see the futility of your own ladders and to find a better way. End your time by listening to or singing your favorite praise song.

GOD AND OUR SHAME

In this section, we explore our Lord's unchanging heart for shame strugglers. We witness a God who persists in love toward his people when he has every reason to turn away. We see a God who is determined to be near and in relationship with the rejected and unworthy. We behold Jesus Christ—the ultimate hope for the broken, weak, and defiled. In him we discover to its fullest extent what it means to be known at our darkest and worst . . . and be loved.

First, we return to Genesis.

DAY 7

He Sees the Unseen

So she called the name of the LORD who spoke to her,
"You are a God of seeing," for she said, "Truly here I
have seen him who looks after me." (Gen. 16:13)

I ONCE ATTENDED a party and ended the night crying in my car. What happened? I was my usual shy, awkward, boring self. It didn't take long before "shy, awkward, and boring" turned into "completely mute and useless to the conversation." I spoke so little at the party that everyone stopped looking in my direction altogether. Eventually they were all happily conversing with their backs turned to me. I still remember the sting of feeling so unseen.

Have you ever felt unseen? You may feel like an outsider at work, at church, or in your own family. There is an "in" group, and you are not in—you feel invisible. Maybe someone else gets all the attention and you are overlooked. Perhaps your well-being was (or is) disregarded, met with chronic neglect or abuse. Perhaps God seems to be blessing everyone except you—and you are left wondering if he has forgotten about you.

In today's passage, we meet Abram and Sarai's servant, Hagar. Abram and Sarai have received God's glorious covenant promise: all the nations on earth will be blessed through their offspring (see Gen. 12:3)—yet Sarai is barren and past the age of childbearing. It seems God's covenant promise won't be fulfilled, so Sarai gives Hagar to Abram to conceive a child in her place. Hagar's pregnancy creates relational strife that leads her to flee into the wilderness. Pregnant, vulnerable, alone in the middle of nowhere . . . Hagar is arguably in a hopeless situation.

Yet it is not hopeless. God sees Hagar when she is alone and in distress. He sends an angel to reassure her in a divine encounter.

29

She will bear her son, and God will take care of them. Hagar matters to him.

Part of the beauty of this story lies in who Hagar is. She's not an important character. She's not the recipient of God's special promise. Abram and Sarai are the important characters here.

So the story of Hagar throws us off, because it expands the scope of who matters *to God*. We wouldn't expect him to go to great lengths to care for the servant woman in the story. We're not sure we expect God to inscripturate this story for all eternity. But he does care about this seemingly insignificant character, and he did preserve this account in the Bible . . . maybe in part to confound our notions of who he cares about, who he sees.

Shame declares, "You do not matter." But God cares about people we're not sure he would care about. He sees those who often go unseen. His gaze is filled with blessing, favor, and care. And we find hope that maybe his watchful regard is for us too . . . for those of us who can also feel small, insignificant, and unnoticed.

Looking back on that party where everyone's back was turned to me, I realize now that there was One who did not turn his back on me. There was One whose face and gaze were directed toward me, just as they were toward Hagar. He says to you and me, "I see you."

Reflect: Can you think of a time when you felt unseen—like you didn't matter? What happened? How did you feel? How did you respond?

Act: As you read through this section of the book, you may feel resistant. The words may feel untrue. Be honest with yourself about how you are responding to Scripture and the reflections. Do you feel comforted? Apathetic? Unbelieving? Take a moment to pray honestly to the Lord.

DAY 8

He Doesn't Give Up on Sinners

And the people of Israel did what was evil in the sight of the LORD. They forgot the LORD their God and served the Baals and the Asheroth. . . . But when the people of Israel cried out to the LORD, the LORD raised up a deliverer for the people of Israel, who saved them. (Judg. 3:7, 9)

ED WELCH, CCEF counselor and teacher, once began a devotional on the book of Judges with the remark "Judges is filled with really, really messed-up people." The sentence still rings in my mind.

If you have read through Judges, you know it's filled with some of the most gruesome and disturbing stories in all Scripture. But the sin that it describes is not only grievous but also cyclical and repetitive. The book's repeated refrain is "And the people of Israel did what was evil in the sight of the Lord." Not once, twice, three times . . . but over and over again (see Judg. 2:11; 3:7, 12; 4:1; 6:1; 10:6; 13:1). They cannot seem to get themselves on track. Dr. Welch was right about these people.

The thing is, if you struggle deeply with shame, you may see *yourself* this way—as really, really messed up. You know other people aren't perfect, but you're convinced your sins and shortcomings are worse. You can acknowledge that other people may also have broken pasts . . . but what happened to you, what you allowed to happen to you . . . the depth of violation, brokenness, and dirtiness seems to be in a league of its own.

Despair seeps into our hearts. We know God loves imperfect, broken, dirty people, but we feel *exceptionally* imperfect, broken, and dirty. The distinction is not just between righteous and sinful. Those of us who struggle deeply with shame feel *especially* sinful. It is not a distinction between pure and dirty. We feel *disgustingly* dirty. Not good. Not even merely bad. *Really, really bad.* When God speaks of his love, we may think to ourselves, surely he isn't talking to people like that—like us.

Is there hope for really, really messed-up people? We read on to verse 9: "But when the people of Israel cried out to the LORD . . ."

We are held in suspense. What happens when really, really messed-up people—repetitively, grievously sinful people—cry out to the Lord for rescue?

"The LORD raised up a deliverer for the people . . . who saved them."

The Lord doesn't give up on them. Rather, he hears their cries. He answers. He intervenes. He comes through. He rescues. Not once. Not twice. Over and over and over again. Today's passage, and the entire book of Judges, show us something utterly humbling: with our God, there is hope for messed-up people. Our God offers hope for *really, really* messed-up people. The ultimate hope and deliverer for our sin and brokenness was yet to come, but even here in the book of Judges we are startled by the God who doesn't give up on us.

Dear believer, perhaps really messed-up believer, you may be so convinced that you're too far gone and beyond his grace. But with our God, there is hope for you.

Reflect: Is there anything about you or your life that causes you to believe you are more messed up than the average person?

Act: In today's passage, the Israelites cried out to the Lord and he heard. I invite you to cry out to the Lord, being honest about your failures and shame. Ask for his help.

DAY 9

He Has Compassion for Dust

*As a father shows compassion to his children, so the L*ORD*
shows compassion to those who fear him. For he knows our
frame; he remembers that we are dust. (Ps. 103:13–14)*

CHRIS LISTED OUT his failures. He wanted to change. But the
past week served as a confirmation that he was no good. He could
have been more disciplined, been more loving, managed his emotions better, been more diligent in prayer and Bible reading . . .

I listened carefully, then chimed in with what may be deemed
an annoying question: "And what about God? What do you imagine is his posture toward you right now?"

I have theories about why this question often elicits eye rolls
and groans. Christians often "know" the right answer to this
question. It's like how in Sunday school the right answer is always
Jesus. We know God loves us. We know we are accepted by God
in Christ. We cognitively know these things are true. Yet so often
there is a disconnect between what we know intellectually and
how we live functionally.

We know intellectually that God loves us. But we functionally live as if he looks on us with love only when our track records
are good—or at least somewhat decent. We know intellectually
that God is gracious and merciful. But how often we imagine that
he is impatient, one failure away from giving up on us. We know
intellectually that God is compassionate. But when we feel frail,
weak—like *dust*—it is hard to imagine the Lord's posture toward
us is one of compassion. Not disdain or contempt. Not prickly
anger and frustration. Compassion.

Once Chris had a chance to reflect, he realized how often he
imagined God shaking his head at him in disappointment and

exasperation. *Come on. What's wrong with you? Get it together. Do better.* He imagined God regretting his decision to choose him as his own, overall displeased and begrudging, ready to leave him behind.

We, like Chris, can imagine many things. What might it look like for us to take today's passage to heart? We have a God of compassion. The compassion of a father who sees and delights in his child who is trying to do his best, even if his best doesn't seem to amount to much. A compassion that says, "Dear child, I know your frame. I know this is not easy for you. I am with you. I will help you. I love you."

Your dust-like qualities—the things that make you feel weak, brittle, frail—feel like reasons for rejection. But it is not so with your Father. His compassion reveals his posture of *favor* toward you. He is merciful and gracious (see Ps. 103:8). His steadfast love is from everlasting to everlasting (see v. 17). Your frailty does not surprise him or cause him to second-guess his relationship with you. Rather, he is moved to help you, eager to come alongside you, committed to bless you, and pleased to reveal more of himself to you in your weakness.

Those of us who struggle with shame need this to be true, don't we? We are dust, and we need a compassionate God. We *need* a God who is gracious, steadfast in love, willing to show mercy in our weakness and failures. We *need* the God of Psalm 103. And, bless the Lord, the God we need is the God he promises to be—whether we fully believe it today or not.

> **Reflect:** What do you imagine is God's posture toward you right now? What did you imagine it was the last time you failed in some way?
>
> **Act:** Write a two- to three-sentence prayer asking for God's grace to enable you to believe and experience the reality of Psalm 103. You can refer to Ephesians 3:14–19 for help.

DAY 10

He Is with You . . . Even There

Where shall I go from your Spirit? Or where shall I flee from your presence? If I ascend to heaven, you are there! If I make my bed in Sheol, you are there! If I take the wings of the morning and dwell in the uttermost parts of the sea, even there your hand shall lead me, and your right hand shall hold me. (Ps. 139:7–10)

SHAME OFTEN LEADS to anxiety. I suppose it makes sense: if you are not good enough, if you are weak and unable, isn't the world a threatening place? If I felt lovable, relationships wouldn't feel so risky; rejection wouldn't feel so inevitable. If I weren't so messed up, self-disclosure wouldn't feel so unsafe. Even the common term *insecurity* ("I'm insecure about how I look") carries a sense of anxiety. You are not secure. You do not stand on firm ground. You are at risk of judgment and disdain.

Shame can lead to many what-if questions:

- What if I do a terrible job?
- What if they all realize I'm an imposter?
- What if he is disgusted when he finds out about my past?
- What if she leaves me for someone better?

We imagine our dreaded outcomes and feel powerless. Maybe if I could do better, *be* better . . . maybe then I could guarantee a favorable outcome. But shame tells me I can't, that I'm not enough, so the worst-case scenario looms. Where are we to find courage when our lives and relationships feel so threatening?

Imagine a current worst-case scenario. What are you scared will happen? What is the scene of catastrophe you envision if your fears were to come true? You may imagine being humiliated, heartbroken, crushed by disappointment. You may wonder if you

35

could recover from the blow. Now ask yourself: Where is God in this scenario? Is he there? Is he active and present to help you? Are you all alone?

In our anxiety, we often forget that we have a God who has committed to never forsake us. That is why Psalm 139 is so precious. It declares that we will never find ourselves somewhere that God is not. It uses extremes to convey the comprehensive totality of this promise. As high as the heavens, as deep as Sheol, from the heights of the sky to the utter depths of the sea, he is present. No matter where you may find yourself—even there, his hand shall lead you. Even there, his right hand shall hold you. Even there . . . in your worst-case scenario.

These realities offer us courage when life feels insecure. God's presence doesn't mean protection from all your feared circumstances and outcomes. It doesn't mean immunity from the heartache of rejection and failure. But it does mean you won't ever be *alone* in those things. Because even there, his hand shall lead you and hold you. Even there, he is committed to writing your story to its ending of full redemption and joy.

Reflect: What areas of life cause you to feel anxious and alone? Can you imagine God with you, holding your hand, leading you, helping you?

Act: Read or sing the lyrics to Jane Borthwick's translation of the hymn "Be Still, My Soul" by Kathrina von Schlegel. Choose a line that resonates with you; write it out and reflect on it.

DAY 11

He Will Never Forget You

"Can a woman forget her nursing child, that she should have no compassion on the son of her womb? Even these may forget, yet I will not forget you." (Isa. 49:15)

WHAT DOES IT feel like to be forgotten?

- A woman with chronic health issues feels left out as she watches her friends on social media enjoy life without her.
- A man is heartbroken after hearing that a woman he had loved found someone new. "She moved on so quickly . . ."
- A mother does everything she can to keep the family functioning. But it has been a while since someone sincerely thanked her or asked her how she's doing.
- A husband and wife realize no one from their church reached out to them during their monthlong absence.

Sometimes shame involves feeling forgotten—a sense of obscurity, a sense that we are disposable. "It doesn't make a difference whether I'm here or not."

Some of us already feel forgotten. Some of us are anxious we *will* be forgotten. Elizabeth Gilbert, author of a *New York Times* bestseller, poignantly shared that writing the book immediately following her bestseller was hard. Even if you are thrust to the top of the top, there is pressure to achieve great things again with the next book, to not fall back into obscurity.[1] We may be tempted to play the ladder game again, but we are trying to find another way.

Consider today's verse from Isaiah. What does God promise? First, he asks the question "Can a woman forget her nursing child?" The implied answer is "No, of course not." Maybe she could forget an acquaintance or her second-grade teacher. But not her nursing child. But in case any doubt lingers, God goes further: "Even these may forget . . . but I will not forget you." You are guaranteed to be remembered by God more surely than a mother remembers her nursing child. Essentially, you are not—and you will never be—forgotten by God.

Has someone ever unexpectedly remembered your name? Isn't it affirming—the fact that you mattered enough for them to remember you? What does it mean that you matter enough for God to assure you that he does and always will remember you? The God of the universe is mindful of you. You live under his nurture and care. Even if you feel lost in a crowd or cast adrift in a sea of faces, whether you feel forsaken today or fear being forsaken in the future, God remembers you. You were never, you will never be, forgotten by him.

Reflect: Is there anyone in your life you feel forgotten by or are scared to be forgotten by? How have you responded to this? Has your approach been helpful or unhelpful to you?

Act: Identify a specific context in which you are tempted to feel forgotten. Ask God to show you a glimpse of his remembrance next time you're in that setting.

He Turns Worldly Standards Upside Down

"Blessed are the poor in spirit, for theirs is the kingdom of heaven." (Matt. 5:3)

"Blessed are . . ."

If you were to finish that sentence for yourself, what would you write? When you think of people who are blessed, what images or words come to mind?

Blessed are . . .

- the beautiful and healthy
- the confident, competent, and charismatic
- the successful and popular
- the happily married with children

Or maybe you think of spiritual things:

- pastors with large, growing churches
- missionaries who witness great fruitfulness on the field
- parents who raise well-behaved children who love the Lord

What are your personal beatitudes?

To be clear, it is good to be healthy. It is a gift to be happily married. Praise God for large, thriving churches. But there is a problem when we narrow our definition of blessedness to these things: we look at our mediocre résumés, our singleness or infertility, our dwindling churches, and then we start to wonder if we are less blessed, less favored—like second-class Christians.

What does "poor in spirit" from today's passage mean? Pastor Martyn Lloyd-Jones writes, "It means a complete absence of pride, . . . of self-assurance and of self-reliance. . . . It is nothing, then, that we can produce; it is nothing that we can do in ourselves. It is just this tremendous awareness of our utter nothingness as we come face to face with God."[1]

If you live in shame, take heart. Jesus's words today are for you. Because maybe you can't "do" competent, charismatic, and fit. Maybe you struggle to "do" happy, healthy, and growing. But maybe you can "do" poor in spirit. And maybe being poor in spirit is the point of our Christian faith.

"Poor in spirit" means that you couldn't, still can't, and were *never meant to* save yourself. It means that you must depend on someone outside yourself. It means you need a Savior. You need Jesus. And feeling your need for Jesus, though painful, is a very, very good—blessed—thing. "Poor in spirit" gives you an opportunity to know Jesus in a way you would never know him if you felt confident and sufficient within yourself. It gives you an opportunity to cling to him in a way you never would if you felt like you could manage life on your own. It gives you an opportunity to cherish and abide in his love in ways that you wouldn't if you felt acceptable and lovable by your own merit.

Poverty of spirit can drive you to resignation and despair. But it can also lead you straight to Jesus. Welcome to Jesus's kingdom. If you are feeling poor in spirit, there is a place for you here.

Reflect: What thoughts or emotions does today's reflection bring to your mind? Are you thankful? Doubtful? How has this reflection reframed the way you think about neediness?

Act: What is one personal beatitude you are tempted to live by? Jot it down. In the coming days, you may find that you instinctively drift away from Jesus's beatitudes and gravitate toward your own. Pray to God for help amidst temptation.

DAY 13

He Really Knows Us

A woman of the city, who was a sinner, when she learned that
[Jesus] was reclining at table in the Pharisee's house, brought an
alabaster flask of ointment, and . . . she began to wet his feet with
her tears . . . and anointed them with the ointment. Now when
the Pharisee . . . saw this, he said to himself, "If this man were a
prophet, he would have known who and what sort of woman this
is who is touching him, for she is a sinner." (Luke 7:37–39)

IT IS ONE of shame's most insidious remarks: "If they really
knew me, they wouldn't love me anymore."

You might spend your life convinced that the only reason
people still like you is that they don't really know you. If they
knew what you were truly like, the sins you struggle with, what
actually happened in your past . . . if they really knew you, the
true you, *all* of you, they wouldn't love you anymore. They would
change their minds about you. They would walk away. Maybe this
has already happened to you.

So you hide and cover up. You pretend. If acceptance and love
are contingent on your ability to keep the ugly parts of yourself
out of sight, hiding naturally becomes your way of life.

Today's passage directs our attention to a sinful woman. She
is not any ordinary sinner. Her life is shameful enough that "sinner" has become her primary identity and public reputation. She
draws near to Jesus to anoint his feet with ointment—and Jesus
receives her. A Pharisee, watching the scene unfold, thinks to
himself, "If [Jesus] were a prophet, he would have known who
and what sort of woman this is" (v. 39). Here we find the all-too-
familiar refrain: "If he really knew . . ."

The Pharisee assumes that the only reason Jesus receives this woman is that *he does not know her*. Yet Jesus knows everything. He knows the sinful woman—her past, her present, her sins, her brokenness, her reputation. In the same way, he knows us—our past, our present, our sins, our brokenness, our reputations. And he does not get up to leave. He does not cast us away. He receives us. He loves us.

This is Jesus. Whatever views we have of him, whatever half-truths we have believed about him, let it be known that our Savior receives shameful, disgraceful, disdained, hurt, and broken people into his presence—and not out of ignorance, obliviousness, or limited knowledge. He knows us fully and loves us nonetheless.

We are often so certain that Jesus has no place or patience for messy, ugly, wounded, imperfect people. Yes, our sins grieve him. Yes, he is committed to changing us. But his posture isn't what we expect. Jesus knows us—as we are today. He knows us—yes, even *those* parts of us. And knowing us, he still wants us to be near him.

Reflect: What parts of your life cause you to say, "If they knew this about me, they would reject me"? What areas of your life do you not want to be known or exposed?

Act: Read Luke 7:36–50. Observe Jesus's posture toward the sinful woman. Notice that Jesus not only doesn't reject her but in fact honors her in everyone's presence.

DAY 14

He Chooses the Unchosen

*For consider your calling, brothers and sisters: not many of you were
wise according to worldly standards, not many were powerful, not
many were of noble birth. But God chose what is foolish in the world
to shame the wise; God chose what is weak in the world to shame the
strong; God chose what is low and despised in the world, even things
that are not, to bring to nothing things that are, so that no human
being might boast in the presence of God. (1 Cor. 1:26–29)*

GOD CHOSE YOU. That is one of the most glorious gospel
realities for shame strugglers. When you see your neediness, your
broken life story, and your ongoing struggles, you are ready to disqualify yourself from his favor and care. But God chose you to be
his—to belong to him, to be his child, to be near him. When you
wouldn't even choose yourself, God chose you.

Imagine the typical scene on the school playground. Two
cool, popular, athletic team captains are recruiting team members
one by one. What do we expect to happen? Don't the other cool,
athletic kids get chosen first? Aren't the scrawny or overweight,
slow, clumsy kids left for last? Don't they feel the looming dread
of being the very last one? That's how the elementary school playground works. And that's how so much of life works too.

That's why today's passage is so surprising, because the apostle
Paul describes a playground scene unlike any other. He describes
a team captain who didn't choose the powerful, high-status, wise,
and strong. Instead he chose the weak, foolish, low, and despised
to be united to Christ and to accomplish his purposes. He chose
the very people who would feel disqualified from being chosen.
Because that is who he is—one whose wisdom exceeds our own,
who continually defies our expectations.

I think of the playground scene once more. Standing in front is the God of all power and holiness; standing in the crowd is needy old me. My head is down, avoiding eye contact, gearing up for business as usual. I brace myself for the inevitable humiliation, knowing full well I am broken and unimpressive and don't have much to offer.

But in the nervous energy and tense silence, he calls out my name. I look up, caught off guard, confused. I look at him, certain I have misheard. But his eyes communicate that he has made no mistake. He says my name again, unwavering. And in the throng of gasps and glances, I slowly, sheepishly, walk toward him. I stand on his side, on his team. In that moment, I am honored and dignified beyond what I could ever deserve. And God, my captain ... he shines so brightly.

Foolish, weak, low, despised, nothing.

Unchosen by the world.

But chosen by God.

Forever united to Christ.

And every ounce of the glory goes to him.

Let the one who boasts, boast in the Lord.

Reflect: Can you picture yourself in the playground scene? Are you surprised that God chose you? If so, why?

Act: Read one passage from the following list: Matthew 8:1–4; 9:10–13; Luke 19:1–10; John 4:1–26. How does Christ interact with the lowly, weak, and foolish of this world? Jot down one or two sentences of reflection.

He Walked the Path of Shame Himself

He was despised and rejected by men, a man of sorrows and acquainted with grief; and as one from whom men hide their faces he was despised, and we esteemed him not. (Isa. 53:3)

"THIS ISN'T HOW you treat the ones you *really* love," I once blurted out to God before I could fully process what I had said. I was suffering, disappointed, and the lie was forming in my mind: God must not love me—this isn't how God treats the children he *really* loves. I thought of other people's testimonies in which God had answered prayers in miraculous ways. In which God's providence, provision, and goodness were so obvious and beautiful. I thought of the Christians I knew who seemed to have picture-perfect lives. "You must really love *them*, God." The doubts grew in intensity, the evidence mounting in my mind that I must be a less-than Christian. Less important. Less loved. Shameful.

But in the escalating chaos of my heart, a gentle question pierced through: "Then what about Jesus?" Our passage today, Isaiah's prophecy about Jesus, flashed before my mind.

Dear believer, what are we to make of Jesus—his suffering, his shame? We know he wasn't "less-than." We don't question whether he was loved by the Father. At Jesus's baptism, the Father boldly proclaims, "This is my beloved Son, with whom I am well pleased" (Matt. 3:17). If we talk about a "less-than" Christian, Jesus is not that. So what are we to make of him?

Today's passage reminds us that Jesus doesn't just speak pleasantries to our shame. He doesn't just promise things, while remaining above the fray, immune, and untouched. Shockingly, he too experienced shame. He endured the eyes of contempt and disdain and knew what it was like for people to turn their backs on him. He was on the receiving end of heartbreaking rejection, abandonment, and betrayal.

When we look at his life, we are forced to rethink our formulas for how to calculate and measure God's love. In the life of Christ, we see a fully pleasing, fully beloved Son who was not spared from the darkness and ravages of shame. The God who permits us to bear our experiences and stories of shame is the God who willingly bore shame himself.

That means that Jesus gets it. He understands. He went before you in your shame journey so that you would never have to walk a single step alone. He is with you *now* as the Great High Priest who sympathizes with you in your struggles.

Jesus rescued us so that shame would not have the final word in our lives. A vital part of that rescue was his willingness to endure his own shame. Shame, suffering, and divine favor all coexisted in the life of Jesus. Perhaps they can coexist in ours too. And if and when they do, Jesus assures us we are not alone. He has gone before us. He goes with us.

Reflect: What is one circumstance of your life that tempts you to believe God must not love you or must love you less than he loves others? How does remembering Jesus's own earthly life and ministry make a difference?

Act: Read Psalm 23. Is there a particular verse that strikes you? You have a Shepherd. You do not walk alone through the valley of the shadow of death—including the valley of shame. Take a moment to choose a verse from this psalm to encourage you today.

He Experienced Shame
on the Cross

And at the ninth hour Jesus cried with a loud voice, "Eloi,
Eloi, lema sabachthani?" which means, "My God, my
God, why have you forsaken me?" . . . And Jesus uttered a
loud cry and breathed his last. (Mark 15:34, 37)

FROM START TO FINISH, the mission of Jesus's life was to obey his Father. He would pour out his life to love and serve the people the Father entrusted to him. He preached, healed, taught, prayed—devoted his life to doing good.

As the Son of God, Jesus was the most glorious man to ever walk this earth, yet he was not treated as such. He was scrutinized, disdained, and misunderstood. He was not born into wealth; he was not reputable and did not live in royal luxury. He was not even respected by the religious leaders of his time. He was so hated by some that they wanted him dead.

In the hours leading up to his death, his very own disciples failed him. Judas betrayed him for money. Three close disciples fell asleep on him in the garden of Gethsemane, despite his pleas for their prayers. Immediately following Jesus's arrest, Peter disassociated himself from Jesus, denying any relationship with him.

Later on, Pontius Pilate brought him before a crowd of people. They could have released him—an innocent man who had devoted his life to doing good. But they didn't. They chose to release Barabbas the murderer. Regarding Jesus, the people repeatedly shouted, "Crucify him."

The soldiers mocked him. Crowned him with a crown of thorns. Saluted as they struck and spit on him.

He was led out to Golgotha. Stripped naked, exposed on a cross for all to see. The people passing by saw him as weak and pitiful, his whole life and identity a sham. "Save yourself, and come down from the cross," they shouted. But there he remained. They didn't know he stayed on the cross to obey his Father.

Exposed, rejected, mocked, disdained, judged, abandoned, betrayed, degraded, humiliated, treated as scum, alone. These experiences are not completely foreign to us. This is shame.

But there was one more disgrace Jesus needed to bear in order to complete his mission—the disgrace of being abandoned by his God as he took our sins upon himself. For our sake, he endured the punishment we as sinners deserved. He endured the agony of divine judgment. He suffered the wrath of the One he had devoted his entire life to. The Father he loved and perfectly obeyed. The Father who loved him. In the last moments of his earthly ministry, alone on the cross, he cried out, "My God, my God, why have you forsaken me?"

Jesus, our Suffering Servant. Jesus, our shamed Savior. Forsaken by people. Forsaken by his Father. Glorious resurrection awaits, but for today we allow ourselves to be sobered by what Jesus endured in order to save us. We consider our own shame— the sting, the heartache, the crushing weight—and realize we have a Savior who understands. We are not alone. We were never alone.

We praise him—because by his willingness to endure shame, he has rescued us from ours.

Reflect: Slowly read through Mark 15 and identify the many ways Jesus endured shame in the final moments of his life. How does that affect you? How do you feel convicted to respond?

Act: Read or sing the lyrics of the 1995 hymn by Stuart Townend "How Deep the Father's Love for Us." Choose a stanza that resonates with you; spend some time with it as you journal or pray.

DAY 17

He Experienced Shame—for Us

[Let us look] to Jesus, the founder and perfecter of our faith, who for the joy that was set before him endured the cross, despising the shame, and is seated at the right hand of the throne of God. (Heb. 12:2)

WE HAVE TALKED about God's surprising posture toward weak, unworthy, shame-filled people. He is not who we expect. The Lord defies our assumptions at every turn—there is a place for broken and unworthy strugglers in his kingdom. He moves toward them and chooses them. He embraces them. This is good news. But today we'll recognize the basis for this good news.

The tension throughout the entire Bible is how a broken, sinful, unworthy people can be restored to relationship with their holy, sinless God. In that sense, the entire Bible is a narrative about shame. Will we ever be good enough? Will we ever be worthy? And the answer for all of us—for all who have sinned—is no. We will never be worthy on our own. Not by our own merit. Because of our sins, we deserve to be forsaken by God.

Except the essence of the gospel is that we do not receive what we deserve. Because Someone else did. Jesus did not endure shame only so he could say, "I know what it's like too." He endured it because it was the only way to rescue us. Because Jesus was forsaken on our behalf, we're not forsaken by God. Because Jesus was rejected, we are accepted. Jesus endured shame because he was on a mission to rescue an undeserving people.

Because these people can't save themselves.

Because there was no other way for these people to find freedom from their shame than for him to take on their shame himself.

Because the only way we can know God's unfailing mercy is for Christ to endure separation and God-forsakenness himself.

Because it was his joy to pave a path of hope for us, even when it meant enduring the cross.

The only true obstacle between you and God was your sin. On the cross, bearing your transgressions, Christ showed his resolve to remove every barrier so that you could enjoy intimate fellowship with him. There is now *nothing* that can separate you from God's love in Christ (see Rom. 8:38–39). No weakness or failure. No abuse. No past mistake. No present or future sin. No hoop to jump through, no mountain to climb—at the cross, no barrier remains to prevent you from enjoying his tender nearness, love, and commitment.

We have a Savior who did everything to ensure that shame does not have the final word in our lives. We experience nothing but good news in our shame because of him, because he stopped at nothing, bearing utter shame himself, to guarantee the outcome of salvation for those who trust in him.

When you look upon Jesus on the cross, hanging by his bloody nail-pierced hands and feet, groaning with thirst, forsaken by man, forsaken by God, for the joy set before him, for you . . . are you still uncertain that he loves you? That he is for you? Is there still any question that he is committed to you and wants you to be near?

Reflect: What is your response to Jesus as you consider that he endured the cross—endured shame—for you? For the joy of saving you and claiming you as his own?

Act: Take a few minutes to review this section on God and our shame. Which day's reflection resonated most deeply with you? Consider writing out that day's verse, memorizing it, or both.

WHAT NOW?

"It is finished," Christ said on the cross. Three days later, he rose from the dead. The mission of Jesus's earthly ministry was complete. Our shamed Savior became our resurrected Savior and is now exalted and seated at the right hand of the throne of God (see Heb. 12:2).

We follow in that same path. Shame will not have the last word in our lives—we too are on the path to honor. What does that path look like? With victory secured in Christ and by the power of the Spirit at work in us, what do we do now?

Accept Christ's Invitation to Rest

"Come to me, all who labor and are heavy laden, and I will give
you rest. Take my yoke upon you, and learn from me, for I am
gentle and lowly in heart, and you will find rest for your souls. For
my yoke is easy, and my burden is light." (Matt. 11:28–30)

IN SOME WAYS this final section is the most important, and potentially the most difficult, part of the devotional. There is hard work ahead. We have stubborn and wandering hearts. Faith requires us to "look not to the things that are seen but to the things that are unseen" (2 Cor. 4:18)—and nothing is easy about that. We have an Enemy dead set against our hope and redemption. Yet our hard work is anchored in the knowledge that we are not left to do this on our own. We do this with Jesus. So this section begins with an invitation from him.

"Come to me," he says. Right now, right where you find yourself. Even if you feel a thousand miles away, oceans apart. Even if a part of you would like to buy more time to clean up your act. Even if shame still leaves you doubtful of God's grace and favor. So much of the power in shame is this sense of isolation. It takes humility and faith to take Jesus at his word and hear his invitation to come to him, when every instinct tells us to stay away.

Perhaps you identify with Jesus's intended audience: "all who labor." Your life may be characterized by anxious preoccupation or slavish toiling and striving. How else will you prove yourself? How else will you measure up?

Perhaps you identify with "heavy laden." You are weighed down by discouragement and pressure. You feel crushed by others' expectations or your own. Your strategies of self-protection and hiding are burdensome. You're lonely. Shame leaves you prickly and defensive when someone says something that hits too close to home. You experience a constant buzz of anxious what-ifs. You're paralyzed. Or maybe you're hypervigilant. You're searching for some distraction, some escape, so you don't have to think about all this.

We turn inward, we turn to others, we turn to things—and this leaves us more weighed down than ever.

So Jesus says to you, "Come to *me* . . . and I will give you rest." Rest from a hamster-wheel existence of trying to earn your way to love and acceptance. Rest from the constant noise of self-loathing. Rest from trying to give everyone the impression you have it all together. Rest from all the ways your shame and your coping strategies have left you exhausted and numb. Rest from a life of self-trust. It is not all up to you. Rest in the arms of a Savior who is gentle and lowly in heart, who extends welcoming, tender care and kindness to you . . . today.

This section may be the most difficult because it requires some *doing* on your part. Jesus makes known to you who he is. Yet you have to take a step yourself: Will you accept his invitation? Will you come?

Reflect: In what ways have you relied on yourself, other people, and things (wealth, status, possessions, entertainment) to achieve well-being in your life? What makes these ways so tempting? How has this reliance left you weary?

Act: You may wonder what "Come to me" looks like practically. For today, write a prayer expressing your desire to accept his invitation. Express your sense of hesitation. Come to him by speaking your heart to him.

DAY 19

Turn to Jesus When
You Feel Rejected

*As you come to him, a living stone rejected by men but in the sight of
God chosen and precious, you yourselves like living stones are being
built up as a spiritual house, to be a holy priesthood. (1 Peter 2:4–5)*

WE CANNOT TALK about shame without talking about other
people. Shame in its essence has a relational aspect. Yes, our relationship with God has *everything* to do with our journeys through
shame. He will never turn away from us. He meets us in our
shame, and Jesus our Savior has borne shame on our behalf. But
what are we to do about other people? God doesn't zap us into
relationship-free lives, a blissful "just-me-and-God" utopia.

We're embedded in relationships—and those relationships
continue to affect us, for better or worse. Faith in Christ does not
mean immunity from rejection—at times stinging, disappointing
rejection. The Lord's steadfast favor does not necessarily spare us
from being hurt and wounded by others.

Peter captures this in today's passage when he speaks of a living stone "rejected by men." He describes the reality that you, like
Jesus, may experience rejection by others in this lifetime.

The temptation for those who struggle with shame is to
believe the words, attitudes, and actions that others direct toward
us. When someone says we're ugly, we're persuaded we are ugly.
When people abandon us, we think we're discardable. When we
witness favoritism and preferential treatment of others, we deem
ourselves deficient and inferior. "Rejected by men" may be an all-
too-familiar reality for some of us.

But "rejected by men" is only one part of today's verse. Peter uses the example of Christ to declare that you may be rejected by men—but in the sight of God, you are chosen and precious. Others may look down on you, turn away from you, overlook you—yet his gaze of affection and delight rests on you.

God does not erase our relationships. He does not spare us from relational disappointment. We may experience shaming, excluding, or dismissive relational dynamics for the rest of our lives. But our God speaks to us *in the midst* of relational disappointment and rejection. He gives us hope that "rejected by men" no longer has sole or final say over our lives. "Rejected by men" and "in the sight of God chosen and precious" can exist simultaneously. He enables us to truly see this.

Your heart may ache. The latest rejection may leave you deflated. God does not call you to be an unaffected, steel-armored stoic in your relationships. But you and I can begin to fight to see what Peter saw, to know what Peter knew: that we, like Jesus, can be rejected by others and chosen and precious—simultaneously.

Knowing that the Lord takes delight in you may not erase your sorrow. But I pray it would remind you there is Someone you can run to *with* your sorrow—because he is with you. Because he cares for you. When you feel rejected, you do not need to endure it alone. The God of all grace and comfort invites you to turn to him and speak to him of your disappointment and heartache today.

Reflect: Reflect on an instance when you were rejected. How did it impact you? How did it shape your view of yourself? How does today's reflection make a difference?

Act: Read Isaiah 53:1–6. Consider how the rejection Jesus experienced provides companionship and refuge for you during rejection.

DAY 20

Come Home to Your Loving Father

*"And he arose and came to his father. But while he was still
a long way off, his father saw him and felt compassion, and
ran and embraced him and kissed him." (Luke 15:20)*

TODAY'S PASSAGE IS from the well-known parable of the
prodigal son. This is the story of a man who dishonored his father
by asking for his inheritance, then squandered it all in reckless living, only to eventually find himself destitute with pigs. His own
decisions wrecked him. He ruined his own life.

When your shame is a consequence of something that is
clearly your fault and you have no one to blame but yourself,
is there hope for you? This may be the most stubborn type of
shame—the type that declares your unworthiness because of
grievous wrongdoing or repeated wrongdoing, failure for the
millionth time. And its declaration is true, and you brought it
on yourself. This prodigal-son kind of shame—does it leave any
hope for you?

I'm confronted with my list of failures today, and I'm not sure
I'm ready to face God either. I feel the doubt. My eyes are lowered. Will he really want to see me? Shouldn't I clean myself up
more? Maybe a few more days of penance, offsetting my sin with
a streak of obedience? I'm not sure I'm ready to stop eating with
the pigs. Maybe you feel the same way.

But good things await us when we approach God. Because
once again, God confounds our expectations. How does a holy
God respond to shame-filled sinners? How does the righteous
Lord respond to failure-ridden, blemished people? Apparently he
sees them when they're still a distance away. Feels compassion.
Embraces them.

Fellow struggler, your hope in the midst of shame is a Person. A Person who delights in your homeward journey. No matter how long ago you left him behind or how grievous your sins have been. Regardless of how many times you chose other things, or yourself, over the One who has done nothing but love you. Your hope is in the Person who, when you decide you don't want to feed with pigs anymore, is waiting for you. The Father who is looking for you will see you from a distance, run toward you, embrace you, and celebrate your return. You don't need to punish yourself. You don't need to earn your way back into the family or make sure *this time* you won't mess it up again. You don't need to stay with the pigs. Your Father invites you, and me—yes, undeserving; yes, spiritually bankrupt—to come home. He receives us when we come home because that is *who he is*.

Not feeling good enough? Welcome to the club. You aren't the first and won't be the last. So come home. It's okay if your eyes are lowered in shame and you feel uneasy. The prodigal son had a whole speech planned out (see Luke 15:18–19). You can have a speech planned out, too, if you would like. Just know that before you say or do anything, your Father will already be running toward you to embrace you, ready to receive you back into the family—and overflowing with gladness that you have come home.

Reflect: What do you usually do after you have grievously sinned? In what ways can you relate to the prodigal son's actions? Does the father's response seem too good to be true?

Act: Read the lyrics to the 1759 hymn by J. Hart "Come, Ye Sinners, Poor and Needy." Choose a stanza that strikes you and spend a few minutes journaling your reflections.

DAY 21

Choose God at the Fork

And the tempter came and said to [Jesus], "If you are the Son of God, command these stones to become loaves of bread." But he answered, "It is written, 'Man shall not live by bread alone, but by every word that comes from the mouth of God.'" (Matt. 4:3–4)

BELIEVER, YOU HAVE an enemy in your shame. And you will need to learn how to say no to him. Let me explain.

For a season in my life, I was drowning in shame. Self-hating thoughts followed me everywhere. At times I managed to distract myself so that they faded to the background. Other times, they were so loud and unrelenting that I felt as though I was in an uncontrollable downward spiral.

This is the downward spiral of shame: when the self-condemnation gathers so much momentum and force that you are convinced it is true. There is no more fight in you to escape or defend yourself. You give in and allow yourself be punched over and over again. "You will never be loved. You are never good enough. Maybe if you were _____, but you're not. You will always be trash. Of course no one loves you." I was in that spiral. The words raced through my mind. The accusations piled on endlessly. My heart pounded. It was hard to breathe.

But that particular night, in the face of these mounting accusations, a word suddenly pierced through: "No."

That was it. One word. "No."

An unfamiliar, Spirit-wrought, miraculous "No."

The reality is, it is not enough to just read about how we are recipients of Christ's kindness and mercy. It is not enough because at some point we must choose to believe these words. We must choose to believe these words are *for us*. We must choose to believe that they are for us, even when every fiber of our being wants to convince us otherwise. And to be clear, they are not merely *for us* but *for you*.

Sometimes shame feels like our only option. But at a crucial fork in the road, we make a decision. Will we choose to believe the word of God, or will we choose to believe ourselves and the Father of Lies—Satan?

Jesus was sent to the wilderness to be tempted by the devil. In today's passage, we see him at his own fork in the road. What will he choose?

Jesus's decision is clear: "Man shall not live by bread alone, but by every word that comes from the mouth of God." He chooses God. Then he chooses God again. And again. Three times in this passage—then thousands more times throughout his life. When faced with a fork in the road, he always chose God—all the way to his death on a cross.

When the lies and accusations of shame fill our hearts and minds, we must fight to say our Spirit-wrought no to Satan, and even to ourselves, so we can say yes to God. It may feel hard, nearly impossible. Pray he would enable you to choose him at the fork.

Reflect: The fork in the road may seem straightforward: "Of course I would choose God over Satan." In real life, it is not so obvious. Can you think of an instance when you were at a fork in the road regarding shame? What made it difficult to believe God's truths?

Act: The act of saying no to the voice of shame may defy everything you have known. Identify a context in which you are tempted to struggle with shame. Consider writing a reminder on a sticky note for you to say no to shame; pray now for divine help to do so.

DAY 22

Build Your House on the Rock

*"Everyone then who hears these words of mine and does them will
be like a wise man who built his house on the rock. . . . And everyone
who hears these words of mine and does not do them will be like a
foolish man who built his house on the sand. And the rain fell, and
the floods came, and the winds blew and beat against that house,
and it fell, and great was the fall of it." (Matt. 7:24, 26–27)*

I WAS SITTING across from my friend when her honest confession came: "I know God loves me. That's great and all. But I want *his* love too." She was referring to the boyfriend who'd suddenly broken up with her the week before.

It's very possible that after hearing the good news of Christ's love you find yourself saying, "Thank you, God . . . this is nice, but there are all these other things that I still want." We may want love and acceptance from a particular person or a group of people. We may still crave recognition, status, or wealth. We may still be gripped by fears, which are often the flipside of our desires—the things we really *don't* want. We don't want to be outshone, rejected, or replaced. Unrequited love is painful. So we anxiously strive and toil for all sorts of things that seem to promise fulfillment, joy, and love.

I don't know what houses you're building. I do know that placing our ultimate trust in other people and their opinions of us, or in any earthly treasure that moth and rust can destroy (see Matt. 6:19)—these are all versions of building our houses on sand. We have a sense of insecurity when we do this. There are no *guarantees* these things will outlast the rain and winds. We are given no guarantees they will stay and abide. Life makes us perpetually vulnerable to risk and loss.

I have built many houses on sand in my lifetime; I've watched many crumble. It has been painful every time. Yet in hindsight, I see this as a mercy, not a curse. The Lord was not being stingy—he loved me too much to allow my hope to ultimately depend on fleeting and unstable realities. He knew I needed to build my house on rock because that's the only place where abiding joy is found. We have the gift of the love of God in Christ—and it is the only gift that cannot and will not be lost. We have a generous Father who knows what we need and cares for us—there is no surer foundation for our souls.

I know your heart may still long for what those houses on sand seem to promise you. It can feel like freedom and joy are found in them. If a day comes when you realize your houses do not bring the joy you hoped for, when you realize they do not cure your struggle with shame, will you hear the Lord's invitation to you? He wants you to enjoy his unchanging, steadfast love and faithfulness, against which no winds or storms will prevail. He wants you to discover the unlosable treasure of himself.

Reflect: Have any of the houses you have built on the sand ever crumbled? Have you ever experienced the joy of being loved, accepted, and wanted—only for those things to disappear? Consider what that was like.

Act: Read the lyrics to the 1787 hymn "How Firm a Foundation." Choose a stanza that resonates with you; take a few moments to write down your reflections.

DAY 23

Serve Others

"But it shall not be so among you. But whoever would be great among you must be your servant, and whoever would be first among you must be slave of all." (Mark 10:43–44)

THE DISCIPLES ARE ARGUING. They desire to be great. They ask Jesus if they may be given seats of honor when he is in heaven—to sit at his right and left hand. In response, Jesus teaches them what true greatness is: to humbly serve. Be a servant to others. Love others.

Consider what Jesus could have said: "But whoever would be great among you must have the most fruitful ministry. Must be competent and powerful. Must feel strong enough to face the challenges of the day. Must have thriving, unwavering faith in all circumstances." We probably wouldn't say any of those things, but I wonder if we live as though they are true. When we imagine greatness, I'm not sure being a servant is on the forefront of our minds.

We can attempt to rid ourselves of shame by ambitiously chasing after self-improvement, status, or wealth. Meanwhile, Christ has prescribed a way forward for us—and it is not to eradicate ambition altogether. It is to be ambitious about the *right* thing. To be ambitious to serve others, to love others, to look out for others' needs and concerns, to move toward them. To offer your time and listening ear, your prayers and encouragement.

David Powlison once talked about the claustrophobic closet of self. Shame can feel this way. We can be consumed with how others see us, with whether we'll be accepted, with how to attain beauty and status, with how to matter. Do you ever feel claustrophobic in that space? Have you ever experienced the fresh air when you temporarily shift your focus away from yourself onto others? When you give of yourself to others, not for any ulterior motive of self-gain, but simply because you are thinking about their well-being? I hope this doesn't sound trite. I just know sometimes the voice of shame fills the entire room of my brain and heart, and sometimes not thinking about myself *at all* has been my oxygen.

As you pursue Jesus's version of greatness, there are no guarantees of favorable outcomes. Loving others is not a foolproof way to become popular and loved. You could be just as invisible as before. You may not be seen as great by anyone else. But you are great to Someone. Someone sees you. Someone notices. Someone experiences pleasure and delight in your every endeavor to serve and bless someone else.

This type of servanthood requires you to live by faith in Christ. He, in fact, paved the way for you: "Even the Son of Man came not to be served but to serve, and to give his life as a ransom for many" (Mark 10:45). The Spirit lovingly conforms us into his image; we follow his footsteps. We step out of the closet of self and give ourselves to others.

Reflect: In the life of Christ, we see someone who loved others more than he was loved by others. We are recipients of this imbalanced love and are invited to follow his lead.[1] Do you remember a time when you sought to love others more than you sought to gain love from others? What was that like?

Act: Sometimes we create elaborate, grand plans. I encourage you to keep it simple. Think of one small way you can serve someone else today.

DAY 24

Love with an Ordinary Love

*If I speak in the tongues of men and of angels, but have not love,
I am a noisy gong or a clanging cymbal. And if I have prophetic
powers, and understand all mysteries and all knowledge, and if I
have all faith, so as to remove mountains, but have not love, I am
nothing. If I give away all I have, and if I deliver up my body to be
burned, but have not love, I gain nothing. (1 Cor. 13:1–3)*

I HAD ONE mission that Sunday morning: "I will love one person. I will ask one person, 'How are you?' and I will genuinely want to know and listen. That's it." The mission emerged out of my struggle with shame: I was getting plugged into a new church, and it wasn't working out. I was awkward. Things weren't clicking, friendships were hard to cultivate, and I blamed myself.

Fast-forward to today. I just received survey results on a recent conference talk I gave. A handful of negative comments are seared in my mind. I suddenly feel ready for an early retirement so I can hide forever.

Serving and loving others is hard when you don't feel like you have much to offer. Each of our cultures (whether societal or specific, such as our particular family or church culture) adopts some value system to rank us and determine the worth of our labors and efforts. For the church of Corinth, it was spiritual gifts (see 1 Cor. 12). People who spoke in tongues and prophesied were deemed superior.

But the apostle Paul disrupts this church's value system. If you speak in tongues but have not love, he says, you amount to no more than a noisy gong or a clanging cymbal. Have prophetic powers, give away everything, become a martyr even, but if you don't have love . . . *you are* nothing.

Love matters most. Not giftedness or charisma. Not competence or even visible success or fruitfulness. Some of us struggle to have a single conversation that doesn't crash and burn in awkwardness. Some of us face health issues that prevent us from being more involved. For whatever reason, we may believe we have nothing significant to contribute. But can you *love* others with the particular, unique, even small gifts God has entrusted to you? Not necessarily fancy, flashy love. Ordinary love. Doing the next small thing. Preparing the meal. Checking in on that one neighbor. Sending a word of encouragement to your pastor. Praying for your friend. Taking a minute to do a favor for your coworker. Asking one person, "How are you?" and really listening. Initiate, pursue, and serve the best you know how to today—in ways that reflect Christ, who initiated, pursued, and served you.

David Powlison said, "Our love for others is at best a flickering three-watt nightlight. But light is light."[1] In darkness, even dim and flickering light matters. There is a dignity to ordinary love. May we commit today to be faithful nightlights by pursuing ordinary, mundane, unimpressive, unnoticed, and imperfect love. It matters.

Reflect: Choose one setting in which you tend to experience shame. Can you articulate the implicit or explicit value or ranking system at work in that setting? How has it tempted you to dismiss your own ability to contribute?

Act: Consider the setting above. What is one way you can plan to move toward and love someone in that setting? What is one small act of love you can do?

DAY 25

Be Honest about Your Brokenness

The saying is trustworthy and deserving of full acceptance, that Christ Jesus came into the world to save sinners, of whom I am the foremost. But I received mercy for this reason, that in me, as the foremost, Jesus Christ might display his perfect patience as an example to those who were to believe in him for eternal life. (1 Tim. 1:15–16)

IT WAS A normal small-group meeting, and we were sharing our prayer requests one by one. "Pray for health" . . . "for patience" . . . "for discipline in Bible reading." Then it was Daniel's turn. "Sorry to be super serious and depressing, but I've been really struggling lately. I'm not doing well." He told us a few more details. We could feel his vulnerability. And all who shared after him felt permission and courage to be more vulnerable themselves.

Because of shame, many of us wear masks in our relationships and ministry. We put smiles on our faces to pretend we are doing better than we are. We conveniently omit certain details of our lives that reveal we are not as put-together as we'd like. We share only the prayer requests that feel safe and socially acceptable. We keep secrets about our pasts so we don't come across as damaged goods. We try to maintain our image as the picture-perfect couple or family, when behind closed doors we aren't. We put forth an image of happiness, strength, competence, or righteousness. Some of us have sophisticated image-management strategies.

Yet in today's passage, the apostle Paul does the opposite. He is transparent about his most grievous failings. He doesn't pretend his shameful past didn't happen. He doesn't announce all his strengths and impressive accomplishments. He acknowledges himself to be not only a sinner but the *foremost* of sinners—the worst of the worst. Yet he does it knowing that his honesty serves as a beautiful testimony of Christ's patience and mercy.

What if part of loving others means allowing them to see the areas of our lives that we often try to hide? What if we follow Paul's lead here? When we share honestly, we create space for other broken, discouraged sinners and sufferers to be honest about their struggles. And our vulnerability becomes a means of displaying the love and worthiness of Christ, who renews our hearts, redeems the broken parts of our lives, and through it all displays his heart of mercy and patience.

Whenever I read Paul's words "sinners, of whom I am the foremost," I always respond with an unspoken "Me too." His words give me permission to acknowledge my own struggles. What would it be like if our churches were characterized less by hiding and pretending and more by the honesty that creates space to say "Me too"? What if our families and communities could be marked by honest confession of sin, by candid expression of emotion and wrestlings—so we could struggle . . . together? And so, through it all, the glories of Christ's mercy could be on full display?

Reflect: Have you ever experienced honesty from someone else about their struggles and found encouragement and strength? Why did it make a difference to you? What do you take away from that experience?

Act: God doesn't ask us to disclose our deepest, darkest secrets to everyone. But he invites us not to deny and cover over the broken parts of our lives. Prayerfully consider how he might be inviting you toward honesty—how your story may serve as a testimony to create space for other strugglers to be honest too. Ask God and trusted loved ones for counsel and wisdom.

DAY 26

Comfort Others with the Comfort You've Received

Blessed be the God and Father of our Lord Jesus Christ, the Father of mercies and God of all comfort, who comforts us in all our affliction, so that we may be able to comfort those who are in any affliction, with the comfort with which we ourselves are comforted by God. (2 Cor. 1:3–4)

"I NOTICED A new guy standing alone at church on Sunday, and I wanted to say hi."

He recounted the story in a very matter-of-fact way, but I knew it was a turning point, even if he didn't see it himself. It was a moment of glory because it was a testimony of shame that had been transformed into love and ministry. *He* was once the guy who stood alone at church. He often felt excluded and overlooked. He hated how awkward and clumsy he was in social situations. He was miserable in his self-loathing; he was depressed and anxious. He didn't know how to make it better. Yet now he was sitting across from me, telling me nonchalantly that on Sunday he had noticed a newcomer standing alone at church and wanted to say hi.

I find that many people who have journeyed with Christ and have experienced his love and goodness in their shame end up here. They begin to notice others who are lonely. They grow in compassion for fellow strugglers. They deepen in their personal conviction to steward their life experiences to comfort others. Although every person's story is different, something is fundamentally profound, true, and helpful about what they have to offer. The apostle Paul himself reminds us that God comforts us in our affliction; now we are able to comfort those who are in *any* affliction. We offer the comfort, the hope—the Redeemer whom we have needed for ourselves. Shame gives way to fruitful, wise, and compassionate ministry.

How God chooses to work in and through us is glorious. He doesn't erase our darkest days of shame. He doesn't grant us amnesia so we forget our most painful moments of loneliness, rejection, and self-loathing. Healing doesn't mean our stories of shame are unwritten.

But our darkest days of shame and our memories of them are transformed into something *good*. Transformed into convictions that grow into fruitful service and eyes that are quick to notice the weak, discouraged, and excluded. Transformed into hearts that are filled with compassion because we know what it's like to feel weak and to reach the end of ourselves. Transformed into mouths that offer beautiful words that speak of the One who is steadfast and merciful. Words that were hard-won, hard-fought-for, hard-earned revelations in our own lives.

Comforting others doesn't require you to have "fully arrived" when it comes to your struggle with shame. But each step forward you have taken, every ounce of comfort you have received, becomes wisdom, direction, and encouragement you can offer to others. Perhaps in the midst of persistent voices that whisper you are broken and not enough—in the midst of ongoing struggle—you too will notice the new guy standing alone at church and want to say hi.

Reflect: When have you been comforted by someone who struggled and didn't have it all together? What was it about their care that resonated with you?

Act: Brainstorm one or two ideas related to how God may be inviting you to notice or move toward others. Start small and simple.

DAY 27

Look for Grace amidst Thorns

Three times I pleaded with the Lord about this, that [the thorn]
should leave me. But he said to me, "My grace is sufficient for you,
for my power is made perfect in weakness." (2 Cor. 12:8–9)

AS YOU WRESTLE with shame, you'll likely discover that it is
really stubborn. It's persistent and convincing. Beautiful words of
love and acceptance may breathe life into your soul, but they can
quickly become flimsy before the bulldozer of shame. You have
been moved by the accounts of Jesus drawing near to the lowly.
Hope glimmers. But it's fleeting. Soon shame clings tightly to
your heart all over again.

The apostle Paul talks about a thorn in his life that he pleaded
for the Lord to remove. The Lord chose not to remove it. Many of
us who struggle with shame resonate with this. It turns out shame
can be our thorn—the thorn that doesn't leave.

We are nearing the end of our devotional. Perhaps you had
imagined your shame would be under control by now, that you
would be further along. Instead, it is possible your life is still characterized by either a mild or a severe sense of failure, worthlessness, and "I'm not enough." If you feel discouraged, I understand.

Sometimes God does not choose to remove our thorn. Sometimes he doesn't answer our prayers the way we hoped. Yet he
promises grace—grace in the midst of unanswered pleas, grace
in the midst of thorns. The challenge for us is to have eyes to see
that grace.

Consider these scenarios. You may still often be flooded with
self-loathing thoughts—but you find you are quicker to turn to
the Lord and pray, "Jesus, help." You text a friend, "Pray for me. I
am struggling." That is grace.

You may still feel self-conscious in social situations. You endure painful, awkward silences; people seem all too content to find polite exits out of conversations. Yet your goal remains: "I will love one person. I will really listen and care." You're more concerned with growing in love for others than with being loved. That is grace.

When you are tempted to emphasize and fixate on only the ways you fell short today, will you also look for evidences of grace? For shame strugglers, identifying and replaying our failures is second nature—as natural and effortless as breathing. Identifying God's grace in our lives, on the other hand, is not.

Perhaps we can acknowledge his grace in epic, dramatic, life-changing events. We love those breakthrough moments. Yet oftentimes God chooses to give grace in small, unimpressive ways. It is grace that you strive to be faithful with that one next thing when shame tempts you to give up in despair. It is grace that you reach out to and love that one person when shame tempts you to believe you are worthless and useless. It is grace when you acknowledge your neediness and reach out for help.

The thorn of shame may persist, but God promises grace that is sufficient—if only we would have eyes to see it. Today, we pray earnestly for eyes to see it.

Reflect: Consider glimpses of grace you have seen in your journey with shame. How does it feel when this happens? Exciting? Disappointing?

Act: Find one piece of evidence of grace in your life today. Do not dismiss it. Be sure to write it down or share it with someone before the day ends. If you are unable to find anything, ask a trusted friend to identify a piece of evidence (and know that the act of reaching out itself is evidence!).

DAY 28

Depend on Others

And they came, bringing to him a paralytic carried by four men. And when they could not get near him because of the crowd, they removed the roof above him, and when they had made an opening, they let down the bed on which the paralytic lay. And when Jesus saw their faith, he said to the paralytic, "Son, your sins are forgiven." (Mark 2:3–5)

IF WE HAVE been in Christian circles long enough, we've undoubtedly been taught the importance of community. The story of the paralytic man isn't the typical go-to passage, but it's helpful for our purposes. It's about a man who is helpless and dependent. He cannot walk. He cannot manage his way to Jesus for healing.

There may be times when shame renders you paralyzed. You feel clouded with self-condemning thoughts. You are convinced you have expended God's grace and there's none left for you. God's promises sound pointless, empty, and untrue. You feel your own lack of resources, lack of faith, lack of strength to fight or even endure your shame. You may feel like you've exhausted all your options. Nothing has worked. This is life as you know it, and it seems as though it will always be this way.

In today's passage, the paralytic experienced a life-changing healing through Jesus. But he didn't get there by himself. He didn't walk himself there or push himself through the crowd. He wasn't the one who climbed to the roof, made an opening, and lowered himself down to Jesus. He didn't, and he *couldn't*. But that wasn't the end of his story. When all he could do was lie in a bed, four men carried him to Jesus. They climbed the roof; they made an opening; they lowered him on his bed. And the passage says that when Jesus saw *their* faith, he said to the paralytic, "Son, your sins are forgiven" (Mark 2:5) and later, "I say to you, rise, pick up your bed, and go home" (v. 11).

There will be days when you'll feel like the paralytic. Some days it will feel like shame has defeated you. It will be hard for you to make your way to Jesus. In my own seasons of shame paralysis, I've needed people to carry me to Jesus, to pray for me when I couldn't manage to pray for myself, to hold on to faith when mine felt weak and battered. I've needed people to believe in God's promises for me when I didn't believe them for myself. Jesus honors that faith.

You were not made to go about this shame journey alone. Pursuing community feels difficult—it violates the essence of shame that drives you into hiding. Perhaps you can ask one person to pray for you this week. You don't have to share *everything*. You don't have to share much of anything. It is enough to familiarize yourself with saying, "Hi . . . I'm struggling. Would you be willing to pray for me this week?" And if nothing else, please know I have prayed for you. You are not alone. We can do this together.

Reflect: Pursuing community is so often easier said than done. What are the obstacles for you? Identifying them may help to provide you with guidance on what to do next.

Act: You may already have people walking alongside you, and I rejoice with you. Or you may feel unclear on your next steps. Would you commit to praying for wisdom and guidance on how you might be able to incorporate trustworthy companions into your journey? Brainstorm one small step you can take toward community this week.

DAY 29

Place Your Hope in Jesus

*"Simon, Simon, behold, Satan demanded to have you,
that he might sift you like wheat, but I have prayed for you
that your faith may not fail." (Luke 22:31–32)*

AS WE NEAR the end of our time together, it is important for us to acknowledge and prepare for potential difficulties we may face in the journey ahead. In today's passage, Jesus foretells Peter's denial of him. Peter is about to face a bitterly hard temptation. Despite his vocal resolve to remain loyal to Jesus unto the end, Peter will not succeed, and Jesus knows it. He tells Peter that Satan has pursued him, demanding to have him. Peter will be sorely tested and come up short. But Jesus has interceded for him so that his faith will not fail.

Perhaps you feel confident, brimming with optimism for the path ahead, or perhaps you feel shaky, unsure if you can really follow through. When we look to ourselves, we may find our own resources insufficient. We want to believe, but we feel our unbelief. Shame feels too powerful; our faith seems flimsy and fragile. We hear the promises of God and intellectually know them to be true, but we don't know how to make these words penetrate our hearts in a way that makes a difference. Some days we feel Satan breathing down our necks, telling us we are disgusting, unlovable, and irredeemable. Maybe we feel sifted like wheat, as though our faith is hanging by a thin thread. It might feel like we are not enough to withstand the Enemy, pursue righteousness, fight the fight of faith.

When these moments come, please hear the words of Christ: "I have prayed for you that your faith may not fail." Yes, you will mess this up. Peter did too. Some days you will find yourself reverting back to old ways. The truths of God's Word will feel impotent and hollow in the face of shame. You will falter, doubt, and languish, and you may struggle to open your Bible, to pray, to ask for prayer. You may struggle to love and serve others. Your soul will move against everything this devotional has spoken of. It will feel too hard. All of it.

In those moments, you will not be able to place hope in yourself to make it right or better. You will gain the sanity that your hope has always been, and always will be, in Christ. Your hope is not in your ability to do everything right but in the One who did everything right on your behalf. It's not in your avoidance of failure but in the One who receives you every time you bring your failures to him. It's not in the quality or frequency of your own prayers but in the One who prays for you.

Wherever you find yourself today, take heart. Your hope is Christ—his power, his presence, his finished work on the cross. He knows the tests, temptations, and trials that await you and has prayed for you in them, that your faith may not fail.

Reflect: Robert Murray M'Cheyne once said, "If I could hear Christ praying for me in the next room, I would not fear a million enemies. Yet the distance makes no difference; He is praying for me."[1] What assurance does it bring in your moments of doubt and failure to hear that Christ is praying for you?

Act: Consider how Satan is tempting you to feel shame today. What is he saying? Does it feel convincing and true? Write down a prayer for grace that will reassure you of Christ's intercession for you in this very temptation.

DAY 30

Persevere in Confidence

And I am sure of this, that he who began a good work in you will bring it to completion at the day of Jesus Christ. (Phil. 1:6)

IF YOU FIND that your shame persists despite your most earnest efforts, know that this experience is normal. To know that it is normal reorients your expectations. What could be interpreted as failure and lack of progress (there is shame again!) is then put in proper perspective.

The apostle Paul in today's passage provides this encouragement to the Philippians. The good work has begun but is not yet complete. However, God will surely bring it to completion one day.

Todd Stryd, a biblical counselor and teacher, uses a metaphor of a voice to describe the experience of shame.[1] With shame, we tend to hear only one voice—the self-condemning, self-hating one—all day, every day. "Not good enough. Ugly. Outcast. Dirty. Unworthy. Rejected. Disposable. Failure."

If the voice of shame is a soloist in our hearts, we must work hard to listen to the voice of truth—God's voice. We may not completely eradicate the voice of shame in this lifetime. Genuine growth might mean that for every ninety-nine thoughts of worthlessness, we are now able to think one thought of God's love.

Not good enough. Ugly. Outcast. Dirty. Unworthy. But *chosen*. Rejected. Disposable. Failure. But *known. And loved.*

Even if the voice of shame continues to clamor at the highest volume, and the voice of God sings only one faint, barely perceptible note, the solo has officially become a duet. Belief has begun to break into unbelief.

As you earnestly seek to trust and abide in the voice of God over time, you may realize the duet eventually sounds different.

The voice of God has steadily grown louder in your heart. A sermon encourages you. A friend's care serves as a tangible reflection of God's heart for you. A passage of Scripture reorients you. Over time, one note of God's voice in your heart becomes two notes, then twenty notes, then fifty notes. You can hear hints of a beautiful melody now, even if incomplete, even if still frequently interrupted by the voice of shame.

And rest assured . . . even if this doesn't happen tomorrow, or in one year, or fifty years, there will be a day when this clashing duet will end. The duet will become a solo again. This time, the voice of *shame* will be extinguished—for eternity. You will stand face-to-face with your God, and he will be the soloist of your heart and soul. No more shame. No more self-condemnation. Only favor, acceptance, honor, and love forevermore. The good work God began will indeed be brought to completion.

Take heart. Persevere. There is an end to this discordant duet. The solo that awaits you will be more glorious and beautiful than any of us can imagine, and it will be your melody forevermore.

Reflect: How does knowing that your struggle with shame is normal reorient your expectation of what progress with shame ought to look like?

Act: Consider a passage that has encouraged you when you have felt ashamed. Write it down or memorize it. When shame attempts to sing solo, reread or recite your chosen passage. Even if it feels unconvincing, rejoice that at least the solo has now become a duet. Every note matters.

DAY 31

Enjoy Glimpses of Redemption

And he who was seated on the throne said, "Behold,
I am making all things new." (Rev. 21:5)

WE END WHERE we began—in Revelation. We've talked about the possibility that our struggle with shame will be life-long. Yet the progress we make in this lifetime is real, true, and beautiful. By God's grace, we grow. We do better at aligning our definitions and measures of success, honor, and worth with God's definitions and measures. We're quicker to confess sin, quicker to turn to prayer. We are less prone to despise or deny our weakness and sin. We share more honestly. We grow in love for others.

Shame tends to create a filter for our lives. We're experts at spotting our sins, failures, and weaknesses. We instinctively fixate on the things we didn't do, the things we did poorly. The things we did—the things we may have even done well—fall to the wayside, forgotten, disregarded, and dismissed.

So we end with an opportunity to intentionally work against this tendency. We have spent thirty-one days together. How do we take inventory of our growth? What are ways we can testify to Christ's work of making all things new—even if that work is incomplete today? What steps have you taken? What inklings of change can you identify?

When I counsel, I often talk about baby steps. Many of us want our growth to be quick, obvious, and grand. We lack vision and excitement for progress that feels slow and small. Yet imagine a baby walking for the first time. She stands with wobbly legs. With trepidation, she takes a quick half-centimeter step, then instantly falls over. She gets back up, only to fall over again within seconds.

These moments are marked by joy, not defeat. Parents respond with delight and excitement, wholehearted claps and cheers. No one condemns the baby for not taking more steps or bigger steps. No one disdains her for walking so slowly or wobbly.

Can we have the same delight and excitement in our own baby steps? Can we acknowledge the grace of God that enables every one of those baby steps? Can we see each step as a testimony of God's faithfulness to us? He has not left us in our brokenness and shame; he has entered in and is committed to making all things new.

This is our journey of hope in our unworthiness: to know the love of our God, to know that his promises are for us, to hope in and live out of the victory Christ secured for us . . . through many, many baby steps.

One day we will reach our awaited destination. All will be redeemed and radiant. We will stand before our God and Savior and behold the one who has known and loved us. We will hear his glorious words of favor, honor, and invitation: "Well done, good and faithful servant. . . . Enter into the joy of your master" (Matt. 25:21). On that day we will be certain that the journey— although hard and at times seemingly impossible—was worth it. Thank you so much for taking this journey with me.

Reflect: Do you tend to overlook or disregard your baby steps? In what ways have you grown in the last thirty-one days? What baby steps have you taken? Are there others who may have noticed a difference?

Act: If there is one takeaway you want to remember from this devotional, what would it be? Take time to write it down. Even better, take time to share it with someone else.

Conclusion

I HEARD THE following story in a sermon when I was a freshman in college. It has brought unspeakable encouragement and comfort to my heart over the years.

There once was a water bearer who walked to the stream every day to fetch water for her mistress. She carried two large pots, one on each end of a pole that rested on her shoulders. One of the pots was cracked. The other pot was perfect. The cracked pot would leak water and was always half empty by the time the water bearer reached her mistress's house; the perfect pot would still be filled to the brim.

This happened for years—the cracked pot delivering only half the amount of water to the mistress's house every day. Finally one day the cracked pot could bear it no more and cried to the water bearer, "I am so sorry and ashamed."

The water bearer asked, "Why are you sorry and ashamed?"

The pot responded, "Because of my cracks, water leaks out of me as we walk back from the stream and I am able to deliver only half a pot of water. Meanwhile the perfect pot is able to deliver a full pot of water every time. I am so sorry."

The water bearer paused, then responded to the cracked pot, "When we walk back from the stream today, I want you to notice the flowers along the path."

As they walked back from the stream to the house, the cracked pot did notice the vibrant flowers along the path and was delighted by their beauty. But when they arrived at the house, the cracked pot was half empty again and apologized to the water bearer.

The water bearer tenderly replied, "Dear cracked pot, did you notice there were flowers on only your side of the path? The thing is: I have always known about your cracks, so years ago I decided to plant flower seeds on your side. Every day as I have walked back from the stream, you have watered these flowers. Thanks to you, I am able to pick the most beautiful flowers to adorn the mistress's house for everyone to enjoy."

Cracks. Failures. Deadweight. Not good enough. Falling short. "I'm sorry for even existing." "You're better off without me. Please just throw me away."

Can you relate to the cracked pot?

I myself have lived so much of my life feeling like a cracked, leaky pot. I've wished I could be more like the perfect pot, the one without cracks, the one that doesn't leak water. I've tried to duct-tape my cracks to stop or at least lessen the leaking. I have tried to become the perfect pot, and it has never worked. I've never succeeded.

When cracks and failures seemed like an inescapable reality of my life, I tried a different strategy. I decided to try to eliminate myself from the game altogether. I decided to sit out. Withdraw. Hide. Play it safe. I was the cracked pot hiding behind shelves and gadgets in the shed so the bearer would no longer see me and use me. *I'm unqualified. Just leave me on the bench, please. Just look away. There's nothing to see here.*

The cracks—it all felt like a mistake. *I felt like a mistake.*

But all the while, God knew what he was doing. He wanted to use the cracks to water the flowers.

This devotional has been about finding hope and courage in the midst of shame. Hope that God can use cracked pots for good. Courage to follow him and be used by him when it seems easier for us to hide and disqualify ourselves. This is part of the God-given journey, the redemptive trajectory in our shame.

So I give up trying to be the perfect pot I never was—and never will be, in this lifetime. I come out of hiding. I write honestly of my cracks and my shame and of the God I've come to know in my cracks and my shame. And as I write, I leak water all over the place. But I continue writing anyway, in hopes that any of these words might splash onto the flowers that God has planted on my side of the path. I write in hopes that Christ's truths and promises that I have learned in and through my cracks and leakiness, the truths and promises I attempt to write here, might provide the smallest amount of hope and comfort to other weary and shame-filled souls. I try to water the flowers.

I imagine there are others like me out there—people with beautiful faith, beautiful stories, beautiful gifts and talents, who see only their cracks, who see only their failures and inadequacies, who can hear or who believe only the voice of shame. All the while, God says, "But I want to use those cracks to water flowers."

This will be a lifelong battle for me. But I try. By the grace of God, I try.

To my fellow cracked and leaky pot, I invite you to do the same. Please try with me. It won't be easy. But there are flowers to be watered. There are people you are uniquely qualified to love and bless—people who will come to know and experience the surprising mercies of Christ through you. There is ministry that God has especially enabled and gifted you to do—not in spite of your shame, but even *through* your experiences of shame. There is a beautiful redemption God longs to accomplish in you and through you, and we pray for eyes to see it and hearts to believe. There are flowers to be watered. I invite you: please water the flowers.

Acknowledgments

WHEN MY BOOK PROPOSAL was accepted in April 2020, I immediately looked forward to writing this section. It felt silly at times to already be thinking about the people I wanted to acknowledge for a book that didn't exist yet. Yet here we are. My heart is overwhelmed with gratitude, because I know this book would not exist apart from the many, many people who walked alongside me through this journey.

First, thank you to my former and current counselees—you have enriched my life. I'm honored to know your stories and have been so inspired by your own journeys toward courage and hope.

Second, I am deeply grateful to the P&R team, including Deepak Reju, Dave Almack, and Amanda Martin. I couldn't have asked for a more gracious, supportive, and skillful team to work with as a first-time author.

Third, I have been so blessed to belong to wonderful communities. To my cherished friends from Westminster Theological Seminary, my former and present colleagues at CCEF, my brothers and sisters from my former church at Crossroads Community Church, and my current church family, Cornerstone Presbyterian Church—my one regret is my inability to name each of you individually. I will never be able to thank you enough for your presence in my life. I will be forever indebted to your unceasing encouragement and prayers throughout this process. So much of what this book is—so much of who I am today—is the fruit of your love.

To Mike Emlet—you have been unwavering in your enthusiasm for my writing, and for me as a person. The words here would have remained buried in files on my computer if it weren't for your encouragement that they were perhaps worth being read by others. Words are not enough to express how grateful I am for your generous love and care for me.

To Ed Welch—I have been edified by your teaching on the topic of shame. But perhaps more important, I have been edified and transformed by your personal support and mentorship. You have always seen more potential in me than I've seen in myself. Your years' worth of encouragement has given me courage. For what feels like a million and one reasons, this book would not exist apart from you.

To my early readers and helpers—Faith Chang, Ruth Chia, Rebecca Eaton, Darby Strickland, and Lauren Whitman—thank you for providing invaluable guidance and encouragement to this first-time author.

To my faithful prayer warriors and cheerleaders over the years—Jimmy Adkins, Sam Alex, Jill Butler, Faith Chang, Sophia Chen, Ruth Chia, Steve Do, Carmen Ewing, Sarah Lee Fung, Alasdair Groves, Hanna Kim, Dan and Jen Liu, Chris McNerney, Andrew Ong, Diana Pak, Deb Peart, Brandon and Jess Peterson, Anne Pettit, Eddie Pyun, Aaron Sironi, Daniella Song, Pau Ping Szeto, and Denise Wilson. There are many more people whose names belong on this list. Please know how grateful I am for each of you. Thank you for believing in me, for persistently checking in on me, and for carrying me to the finish line.

A special thank-you to my family: my mom, Su-lien Chen, my brother and sister-in-law, Victor and Shirley—and my two favorite girls in the world: Reagan and Avery.

Lastly, to my former professor and boss, David Powlison, and to my father, Jung-Chao Liu—I cannot deny my sadness that you are not here to celebrate this moment with me. But I take heart knowing that the imprints of your life and love are everywhere in this book. I hope I have made you proud. Thank you for everything.

Notes

Day 3: "I Must Hide"

1. Timothy Keller with Kathy Keller, *The Meaning of Marriage: Facing the Complexities of Commitment with the Wisdom of God* (New York: Dutton, 2011), 95.

Day 5: "I'll Try Harder"

1. See David Powlison, *Good and Angry: Redeeming Anger, Irritation, Complaining, and Bitterness* (Greensboro, NC: New Growth Press, 2016), 207–14.
2. Powlison, 211.

Day 11: He Will Never Forget You

1. See Elizabeth Gilbert, "Success, Failure and the Drive to Keep Creating," filmed March 2014 in Vancouver, BC, TED video, 7:05, https://www.ted.com/talks/elizabeth_gilbert_success_failure _and_the_drive_to_keep_creating.

Day 12: He Turns Worldly Standards Upside Down

1. D. Martyn Lloyd-Jones, *Studies in the Sermon on the Mount: Matthew 5:1–48* (Grand Rapids: Eerdmans, 1960), 50.

Day 23: Serve Others

1. See Edward T. Welch, *A Small Book about Why We Hide: How Jesus Rescues Us from Insecurity, Regret, Failure, and Shame* (Greensboro, NC: New Growth Press, 2021), 53.

Day 24: Love with an Ordinary Love

1. David Powlison, *Good and Angry: Redeeming Anger, Irritation, Complaining, and Bitterness* (Greensboro, NC: New Growth Press, 2016), 82.

Day 29: Place Your Hope in Jesus

1. Andrew A. Bonar, *Memoir and Remains of the Rev. Robert Murray M'Cheyne* (repr., Edinburgh, 1894), 158.

Day 30: Persevere in Confidence

1. See Todd Stryd, "I often don't feel good enough. How do I grow when the voice of shame is so convincing?" CCEF, May 21, 2020, www.ccef.org/video/i-often-dont-feel-good-enough-how-do-i-grow-when-the-voice-of-shame-is-so-convincing.

Suggested Resources
for the Journey

Langberg, Diane Mandt. *On the Threshold of Hope: Opening the Door to Hope and Healing for Survivors of Sexual Abuse.* Carol Stream, IL: Tyndale House, 1999. [For those who experience shame due to sexual abuse, Langberg offers compassionate and wise words that guide you toward healing and light.]

Ortlund, Dane. *Gentle and Lowly: The Heart of Christ for Sinners and Sufferers.* Wheaton, IL: Crossway, 2020. [This is a beautiful book for anyone who would like to learn more deeply the heart of God amid your failures and shortcomings.]

Welch, Edward T. *Shame Interrupted: How God Lifts the Pain of Worthlessness and Rejection.* Greensboro, NC: New Growth Press, 2012. [Welch provides a robust and rich description and biblical understanding of the experience of shame. If you are interested in deepening your knowledge of how Scripture speaks to shame, I highly recommend this resource.]

———. *Side by Side: Walking with Others in Wisdom and Love.* Wheaton, IL: Crossway, 2015. [Welch has written a pivotal book on what it looks like to walk wisely as needy and needed people. If you are interested in both theological and practical vision for faithful and wise ministry among ordinary people, I cannot recommend this resource enough.]

Restoring Christ to Counseling and Counseling to the Church

COUNSELING
ccef.org/counseling

WRITING
ccef.org/resources

TEACHING
ccef.org/courses

EVENTS
ccef.org/events

"CCEF is all about giving hope and help with a 'heart.' If you want to learn how to effectively use God's Word in counseling, this is your resource!"

Joni Eareckson Tada, Founder and CEO, Joni and Friends International Disability Center

"The vision of the centrality of God, the sufficiency of Scripture, and the necessity of sweet spiritual communion with the crucified and living Christ–these impulses that lie behind the CCEF ministries make it easy to commend them to everyone who loves the Church."

John Piper, Founder, desiringGod.org; Chancellor, Bethlehem College & Seminary

Christian Counseling & Educational Foundation
ccef.org

More Help for Your Thought Life from P&R Publishing

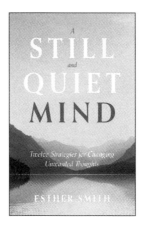

Do you ever feel bombarded with unwanted thoughts? God has given you many different ways to calm your mind and live at peace. In this practical and sympathetic guidebook, biblical counselor Esther Smith provides twelve powerful strategies to help you. Each chapter is filled with a variety of exercises so that you can begin the process of changing your thoughts right away.

"Esther Smith has written the most practical and biblically faithful book on navigating unwanted thoughts that we have ever encountered. Her combination of compassion and creativity makes it feel as though she is stepping from the pages of the book, putting her arms around the reader, and leading them personally through exercises toward real change."
—**David and Krista Dunham**, Counselors

"Many of my counselees wrestle with untrue thoughts about themselves, the world, and the Lord. Esther has written a comprehensive and compassionate resource that they can engage as a workbook to reorient their hearts to God's precious truths."
—**Darby A. Strickland**, Counselor

Did you find this book helpful?
Consider leaving a review online.
The author appreciates your feedback!

Or write to P&R at editorial@prpbooks.com
with your comments. We'd love to hear from you.